GLUTEN-FREE & VEGAN

for the

whole family

GLUTEN-FREE & VEGAN

for the

whole family

Nutritious Plant-Based Meals and Snacks Everyone Will Love

JENNIFER KATZINGER

Foreword by Raven Bonnar-Pizzorno

Photographs by Charity Burggraaf

SASQUATCH BOOKS
SEATTLE

Printed in China

Published by Sasquatch Books
19 18 17 16 15   9 8 7 6 5 4 3 2 1

Editor: Susan Roxborough
Project editor: Em Gale
Design: Anna Goldstein
Illustrations: Joyce Hwang
Photographs: Charity Burggraaf
Food styling: Julie Hopper
Copy editor: Kristi Hein

Library of Congress Cataloging-in-Publication
Data is available.

ISBN: 978-1-57061-955-7

Sasquatch Books
1904 Third Avenue, Suite 710
Seattle, WA 98101
(206) 467-4300
www.sasquatchbooks.com
custserv@sasquatchbooks.com

For my daughter, Lillian

CONTENTS

RECEIPE LIST

FOREWORD

Food is our foundation, providing nutrients for our health to thrive, and is the centerpiece of many of our celebrations. This book honors the diverse and vital role food plays in our lives, and is a great resource for nutritious eating for people who want to increase the amount of plant-based foods they eat.

Research tells us that making the majority of our meals plant-based helps protect us against many of the chronic diseases that face modern societies, such as diabetes, heart disease, and many cancers. Plant-based diets made up of nutrient-dense meals, such as the ones described in this book, are high in fiber, folate, magnesium, potassium, and vitamins C and E, and lower in cholesterol and saturated fat.

It is the position of the Academy of Nutrition and Dietetics, the world's largest organization of food and nutrition professionals, that "appropriately planned vegetarian diets, including total vegetarian or vegan diets, are healthful, nutritionally adequate, and may provide health benefits in the prevention and treatment of certain diseases. Well-planned vegetarian diets are appropriate for individuals during all stages of the life cycle, including pregnancy, lactation, infancy, childhood, and adolescence, and for athletes." To this end, Jennifer focuses on including foods that are high in nutrients that can be hard to get in gluten-free or vegan diets. She combines vegan protein sources in recipes to create complete proteins, or recommends foods to pair that will complete the protein.

What about the health-promoting vitamins, minerals, and phytonutrients that aren't household names and are lacking in the diets of most modern eaters? Nutrient-dense whole foods provide a wealth of these nutrients, and Jennifer creates delicious, healthy recipes that the whole family can enjoy. Her recipes are high in mono-unsaturated fats from olive oil and avocado, and omega-3 fat sources like walnuts, flaxseeds, and chia seeds.

Through Jennifer's recipes we discover new ways to include nutritional superstars in our daily meals. Iron is found throughout this book in raisins, prunes, and black strap molasses. These recipes are full of whole grains, beans, nuts, and yeast that provide the mineral zinc. While many people who eat gluten-free do not get adequate amounts of fiber, most of Jennifer's recipes are high in blood sugar–stabilizing and colon-cleansing fiber. And this book is full of good sources of calcium like almonds, chia seeds, and tofu.

Jennifer's specialty is desserts free of common allergens and sweetened with unrefined sugars—*wow*! Baking can be complex, and anyone who has tried to replace eggs, butter, or wheat with an alternative knows it can turn out to be a flop. But here, Jennifer has taken the guesswork out of it with hours of testing and over a decade of professional gluten-free and vegan baking and recipe development experience. And, her dessert recipes honor the tradition of people coming together around food by providing treats that even people with allergies to eggs, wheat, gluten, and dairy can enjoy and not feel left out.

These delicious recipes are a foundation for healthy eating for the whole family, young and old, and for those with or without food allergies. I am lucky to call Jennifer a friend and to live in Seattle where I could go to her bakery with friends and family. Join Jennifer in her enthusiasm and love of cooking to nourish yourself and your family.

RAVEN BONNAR-PIZZORNO, MS, RD, CD
Registered Dietitian

INTRODUCTION

Researching and writing about the nutritional information in this cook-book has been absolutely fascinating. For every single ingredient, one can find pages upon pages of compelling studies of how foods impact the quality and health of our lives. Summarizing what health data stood out the most to me in the notes for each recipe was truly challenging, but I hope it is just enough to whet your appetite for further delving into the nutritional details. You can use this book as a stepping-stone at the beginning of your journey in appreciating just how amazing food is and how food can truly be medicine. My favorite websites to visit in my research are first and foremost The World's Healthiest Foods, as well as How Stuff Works and Organic Facts.

Before I took this project on, I had always considered myself pretty knowledgeable about health. I had a very confident yet (as it turned out) superficial understanding that antioxidants and anti-inflammatories were good; eating lots of vegetables was cancer preventive; in general it was healthier to avoid sugar; it's important to include omega-3s; we should eat fermented foods; kids need plenty of protein, iron, and mineral-rich foods; eating lots of fiber prevents diabetes; and so on. Now I can say that all of these are certainly validated in the existing studies, and I have a much deeper understanding of the facts.

I'd like to emphatically state that this book is for everyone! You do not have to be gluten-free or vegan to enjoy this book. Everyone will benefit from these tasty meals, and you will soon see why as you explore the recipes. If you or a family member have intolerances, allergies, or an inflammatory disease, this book will be very helpful, as it avoids most allergens (all the recipes are gluten-, dairy-, and egg-free, and mostly soy-free—just two recipes contain soy—and very few recipes use corn). In addition, the desserts are sweetened mainly with dates and phenol-rich maple syrup. Also, eating a mostly plant-based diet is a preventive measure for avoiding many diseases down the road for people of all ages. I do not advise that everyone should eat only plant-based foods; however, I do believe that the more plant-based foods (and the fewer processed foods) we incorporate into what we eat, the better off we will be with regard to preventing diabetes, cancers, immune disorders, and inflammatory diseases. Plus, we will feel better and have more energy. I know that when I feel good and have energy, I am generally happier. I think you'll make the same discovery.

So how is it that whole plant foods are so powerful? In a nutshell, plants are constantly responding to their environments, and when we eat those foods we gain from the information encoded by the plants, which helps our systems likewise respond to environmental stresses, such as pollutants, toxins, bacteria, and viruses. Whole plant foods are made of phytonutrients; there are 25,000 known phytonutrients—chemicals found only in plants! These phytonutrients communicate with enzymes in our bodies, constantly working to protect us from outside stresses and safeguard against cancers, reduce inflammation, preserve eye health, and reduce the risk of heart disease. Whole foods are composed of a complex assemblage of balanced nutrients in perfect design that cannot come close to being reproduced by a supplement! (That is not to say

Many of the recipes in this book, such as the vegetable stock and nut milk, are also used throughout other recipes as ingredients. While I believe that unprocessed, homemade foods are the best quality, if you're in a pinch or wanting a quick dinner, feel free to substitute any of these ingredients with store-bought items.

there is no place for supplements; indeed, they can restore balance and fill nutritional gaps. Notably, vegans must be aware of their vitamin B12 levels and are encouraged to take supplemental B12.) Whole plant foods are likewise lavish in soluble and insoluble fiber that slows down digestive transit time, making it possible to absorb more nutrients from the foods; this fiber also influences our blood sugar level for the better and prevents conditions of imbalance such as diabetes. Simply put, if we take care of ourselves by predominantly eating whole plant foods, avoiding common pollutants such as pesticides or plastics, exercising moderately, and living balanced lives, we can protect ourselves even if we're genetically at risk.

Finally, I know that making meals for the family that meet everyone's needs and tastes can be challenging sometimes. I've designed these recipes so you can make family-friendly dishes with the comforting appeal of traditional meals. They are full of essential nutrients, especially protein and iron, and not too spicy. And of course they are mouthwateringly delish and fun to eat. Food truly matters! I know, from raising my own daughter in a society in which eating genetically modified, plastic packaged, processed foods is the norm, that it can be daunting to establish balance in our social eating when the pendulum has swung so far away from health. My hope is to shed some light on the exquisiteness of whole plant foods and our dependence on them for healthy living.

staples

IN THIS CHAPTER, you'll find two bread recipes; in particular, the Quinoa Flatbread (page 8) is particularly high in protein and is a fantastic accompaniment to any soup or salad recipe. Try leaving the homemade Walnut Almond Milk (page 18) unstrained for the added benefit of additional fiber. I also recommend using the Vegetable Stock (page 19) instead of water when cooking savory grains, to further boost nutrition.

Along with these staples, there are a variety of fermented nut cheese recipes, like the Herbed Soft Cheese (page 12), as well as Nut Milk Yogurt (page 10), which is creamy and delicious. Fermentation in foods occurs when natural bacteria eat sugars and starches and in doing so create lactic acid. This helps to preserve the food and its nutrients, while also producing health-promoting enzymes, omega-3 fatty acids, B vitamins, and a variety of probiotics. Because fermentation breaks down food, it becomes much more digestible and is abundant in immunity-boosting chemicals that combat harmful bacteria and even cancer cells.

sandwich bread

This sandwich bread has three super sources of protein: quinoa, teff, and gluten-free oats. This lovely bread will find a place in so many meals. You can make it into buns too—a superb way to enjoy a bean burger. When you are pressed for time, a familiar nut butter sandwich on this protein-rich bread really hits the spot!

Makes 1 loaf

1¾ cups brown rice flour,
   plus more for dusting
½ cup quinoa flour
½ cup teff flour
½ cup tapioca flour
1 cup gluten-free oats

1 teaspoon kosher salt
2 teaspoons xanthan gum
¼ cup canola oil
¼ cup maple syrup
1½ cups warm water
1 package active dry yeast

1. Preheat the oven to 375 degrees F.

2. In a medium mixing bowl, combine the flours, oats, salt, and xanthan gum. Set aside.

3. In the bowl of a stand mixer fitted with the paddle attachment (or in a large mixing bowl by hand with a wooden spoon), combine the oil, maple syrup, water, and yeast. When the yeast starts bubbling, mix in the dry ingredients. The dough will come together within about 1 minute (or 2 to 3 minutes by hand).

4. Lightly dust a work surface with brown rice flour and gently shape the dough into an oblong loaf to fit into a parchment paper–lined 8-by-4-inch bread pan, or make a round loaf and put it on an unoiled baking sheet. Gently score the bread and bake until the top is golden and firm, about 55 minutes. Cool, then wrap the bread in parchment paper and seal in a ziplock bag. Store in the refrigerator for up to 4 days.

quinoa flatbread

Quinoa is a complex carbohydrate and will provide lasting, balanced energy without producing sugar spikes and lows. It is also a complete protein! This flatbread pairs so tastily with the Red Bean Hummus (page 73). I find this flatbread is most enjoyable when eaten within two days, and it is a real treat served warm, especially when dipped in a high-quality extra-virgin olive oil. Spread with a soft nut cheese for an afternoon snack.

Makes 8 flatbreads

Brown rice flour, for dusting
2½ cups quinoa flour
½ cup teff flour
¾ teaspoon baking soda

1 teaspoon sea salt, plus more
   for sprinkling
¼ cup canola oil
⅛ cup maple syrup
1 cup water

1. Preheat the oven 375 degrees F.

2. Line 2 baking sheets with parchment paper and dust with brown rice flour. In the bowl of a stand mixer fitted with the paddle attachment (or in a large mixing bowl by hand with a wooden spoon), combine all the ingredients, mixing thoroughly until a smooth dough is formed.

3. Generously dust a work surface with brown rice flour and coat your hands as well. Divide the dough into 8 equal portions, about ¼ cup each, and work into balls. Put the balls of dough on the baking sheets, 4 per pan, leaving ample space between each. Re-coat your hands with brown rice flour and flatten the balls to about 5 inches in diameter and ¼ inch thick. Sprinkle with additional salt if desired. Bake until golden and firm to the touch, about 15 minutes. Cool, then wrap the bread in parchment paper and seal in a ziplock bag. Store in the refrigerator for up to 2 days.

For a time saver, consider making the dough the night before you want to bake it. Store the divided rounds, rolled in brown rice flour, in a sealed container in the refrigerator. In the morning, simply preheat the oven and shape, flatten, and bake the flatbreads. Wrapped in foil, the finished flatbreads retain their heat for a lovely warm treat in a packed lunch. Try a culinary adventure—these flatbreads are easy to dress up with a variety of spices or herbs. Brush the unbaked flattened dough with extra-virgin olive oil and salt. For spices, sprinkle with sumac, paprika, cumin, crushed coriander, or curry. Dried or fresh herbs such as rosemary, oregano, basil, and even chopped garlic are also scrumptious.

nut milk yogurt

Creamy yogurt is a wonderful way to start any day (especially combined with homemade muesli). It also serves up as a satisfying snack. This particular nut milk yogurt is rich in healthy probiotics and raw nuts. The nuts, so full of minerals, make this delicious staple a great bone-building treat, and the healthy bacteria boost the immune system. Yogurt parfaits, mixed up with fresh berries and a tad of maple syrup, make a pretty fancy dessert too! If you're using probiotic capsules, make sure to use enough to provide thirty-five to forty billion CFUs (colon-forming units); refer to the packaging.

Makes about 2 quarts

1 cup raw almonds
½ cup raw walnuts
½ cup raw macadamia nuts
  or almonds
7 cups filtered water, divided
¼ cup arrowroot powder

1 teaspoon agar-agar powder
1½ tablespoons maple syrup
Heaping ⅛ teaspoon probiotic
  powder (contents of about
  1 capsule)

1. Put the nuts in a large sealable container and cover with water. Cover and put in the refrigerator for 8 to 12 hours.

2. Prepare your tools (see note) by sterilizing the pitcher portion of the blender, straining bag, measuring cups, measuring spoons, whisk, and fermentation containers in simmering water.

3. Rinse the nuts well and drain. In the blender, blend the nuts and 1½ cups of the water until smooth. Put the straining bag over a large bowl and pour the nut slurry through. Clean the pitcher and return the strained liquid to it. Add 2 cups of the water to the pitcher and set aside.

4. In a small bowl, whisk the arrowroot powder with ½ cup of the water and set aside.

5. In a large pot, add the remaining 3 cups water. Sprinkle the agar-agar powder over the surface of the water and simmer for 4 minutes, or until the agar-agar is completely dissolved.

6. Whisk the strained liquid and maple syrup into the agar-agar mixture. Return to a simmer, stirring occasionally. Whisk in the arrowroot mixture (rinse out the small bowl and set aside) and simmer for no longer than 12 seconds. Immediately remove from the heat.

7. Let the mixture cool to 100 to 105 degrees F, about 45 to 90 minutes (use a thermometer to test).

8. Remove a cup of the mixture to the small bowl and mix in the probiotic powder. Add this back to the rest of the mixture and whisk well.

9. Pour the mixture into the fermentation containers. Seal well and put in the cooler. Pour warm water around the containers so it reaches almost to the top of the containers. Cover the cooler tightly and wrap with a blanket to insulate. Allow the yogurt to ferment in the cooler until a thick, creamy consistency is achieved, about 10 hours. Transfer the containers to the refrigerator and store for up to 2 weeks.

TOOLS YOU'LL NEED:
- Blender
- Straining bag
- Measuring cups (¼ cup, ½ cup, and 1 cup)
- Teaspoon
- Tablespoon
- Whisk
- 10 (1-cup) or 2 (1-quart) fermentation containers (such as empty glass jam jars or canning jars)
- Insulated cooler

herbed soft cheese

This scrumptious fermented yet mild soft cheese is high in fiber and healthy fats. I call for this cheese in the TLT Sandwich (page 49). It also makes a great dip with crudités and spreads smoothly on crackers or flatbread. The Brazil nuts provide selenium, which boosts the immune system and aids the absorption of vitamin E. Please note you will need cheesecloth. Feel free to omit the black pepper and herbs for an even milder cheese.

Makes 20 ounces

1 cup blanched almonds
¼ cup macadamia nuts
¼ cup Brazil nuts
¼ cup pine nuts
1 teaspoon probiotic powder
    (contents of about 6 capsules)
1 tablespoon plus 2 teaspoons
    nutritional yeast
2 teaspoons onion powder

Pinch of freshly grated nutmeg
1 teaspoon sea salt
Freshly ground black pepper
1 tablespoon finely chopped
    fresh chives
1 tablespoon finely chopped
    fresh thyme
1 tablespoon finely chopped
    fresh oregano

1. Put the nuts in a large sealable container and cover with water. Cover and put in the refrigerator overnight, or for 12 to 14 hours.

2. Rinse the nuts well and drain. In a food processor or blender, blend the nuts with the probiotic powder. Blend thoroughly, taking time to scrape down the sides of the food processor to ensure the entire mixture is pureed to a very smooth consistency.

3. Prepare 3 layers of cheesecloth by rinsing them and then layering in a fine mesh strainer over a large bowl; there should be ample overhang. Put the nut mixture in the cheesecloth. Gather the cheesecloth around the nut mixture and twist the cloth, forming a ball. Secure the closure with string or a twist tie and keep the strainer over the bowl to capture drainage. Fill a clean gallon container with water and set it directly on the cheesecloth ball. This weight will help to separate the liquid from the nut mixture to create a firmer cheese. Set in a warm place to culture for 14 to 16 hours.

4. Discard the extracted liquid. In a medium bowl, stir together the cheese, nutritional yeast, onion powder, nutmeg, salt, pepper, chives, thyme, and oregano. Store the cheese in an airtight container in the refrigerator for up to 5 days.

> To make a fancy presentation, perhaps for a dinner party, spread the herbs with a good grinding of pepper on a sheet of parchment paper. Form the cheese into a log about 4 inches long by 1½ inches in diameter. Roll the log across the herbs to coat. Serve the cheese log presliced into rounds or whole with a spreading knife.

cream cheese

This smooth, mild cheese is made predominantly of cashews. Cashews contain very high amounts of magnesium and copper—superstars when it comes to building bone strength and flexibility. For a treat, we like to spread this cream cheese on bread and top with berry jam. The cheese can also be piped into cherry tomatoes for a fancy appetizer. Please note you will need cheesecloth.

Makes 20 ounces

1¼ cups cashews
½ cup almonds
¼ cup pine nuts
1 teaspoon probiotic powder
   (contents of about 6 capsules)

1 tablespoon plus 2 teaspoons
   nutritional yeast
Pinch of freshly grated nutmeg
1 teaspoon sea salt

1. Put the nuts in a large sealable container and cover with water. Cover and put in the refrigerator overnight, or for 12 to 14 hours.

2. Rinse the nuts well and drain. In a food processor or blender, blend the nuts with the probiotic powder. Blend thoroughly, taking time to scrape the sides of the food processor to ensure the entire mixture is pureed to a very smooth consistency.

3. Prepare 3 layers of cheesecloth by rinsing them and then layering in a fine mesh strainer over a large bowl; there should be ample overhang. Put the nut mixture in the cheesecloth. Gather the cheesecloth around the nut mixture and twist the cloth, forming a ball. Secure the closure with string or a twist tie and keep the strainer over the bowl to capture drainage. Fill a clean gallon container with water and set it directly on the cheesecloth ball. This weight will help to separate the liquid from the nut mixture to create a firmer cheese. Set in a warm place to culture for 14 to 16 hours.

4. Discard the extracted liquid. In a medium bowl, stir together the cheese and the nutritional yeast, nutmeg, and salt. Store the cheese in an airtight container in the refrigerator for up to 2 weeks.

For a sweet treat, I omit the nutritional yeast. Instead, I whip ⅓ cup maple syrup into the cheese after it has cultured. This makes for a delicious frosting-like consistency that we enjoy spreading on warm muffins. You can even dip fresh fruit slices into the cheese for a dessert-like fondue.

almond feta cheese

A feta cheese in the refrigerator comes in handy for sprucing up salads and pizzas! In this recipe, the feta is made predominantly of almonds and pine nuts. Almonds contain nutrients such as riboflavin and acetyl-L carnitine, which increase brain activity, as well as phosphorus, which is essential for building strong bones and teeth. Pine nuts are a great source of iron. Feel free to omit the herbs if you prefer a plain feta in order to have a wider variety of foods to pair with. I love filling half of a date with plain feta! Please note you will need cheesecloth.

Makes two 10-ounce rounds

1 cup almonds
1 cup pine nuts
½ cup freshly squeezed lemon juice
6 tablespoons extra-virgin olive oil
2 cloves garlic

1 tablespoon chopped fresh basil
2 teaspoons chopped fresh oregano
2½ teaspoons sea salt
1 cup water

1. Put the nuts in a large sealable container and cover with water. Cover and put in the refrigerator for 24 hours.

2. Rinse the nuts well and drain. In a food processor or blender, blend the nuts with the lemon juice, oil, garlic, basil, oregano, salt, and water until very smooth and creamy.

3. Prepare 3 layers of cheesecloth by rinsing them and then layering in a fine mesh strainer over a large bowl; there should be ample overhang. Put the nut mixture in the cheesecloth. Gather the cheesecloth around the nut mixture and twist the cloth, forming a ball. Twist as much as possible to squeeze out the moisture. Discard the extracted liquid. Secure the closure with string or a twist tie. Refrigerate the secured ball in the strainer over the bowl overnight. In the morning, discard any separated liquid.

4. Preheat the oven to 200 degrees F.

5. Unwrap the cheesecloth and divide the cheese ball into 2 equal portions. Line 2 baking sheets with parchment paper. Flatten each cheese portion into a disk directly on the parchment. Each disk should be ¾ inch thick. Bake for 40 minutes. Cool, then store the cheese in an airtight container in the refrigerator for up to 2 weeks.

Growing your own potted herbs indoors on a kitchen windowsill is so easy to do and allows one to have otherwise seasonal herbs year-round. Having fresh herbs at your fingertips brings the delightful opportunity to add brightness and interest to the palette in a myriad of applications. Whether it be herbal iced tea, a garden salad, a savory bean dish, or homemade cheeses, fresh herbs can change a bland food into something dynamic. To grow your own, make sure to pick a window with plenty of sunlight!

walnut almond milk

Having homemade dairy-free milks on hand is a delight because, for one thing, they are really a cinch to make, and for another, they are free of all those strange gums, starches, and "natural flavors" that are hard to avoid in store-bought dairy-free milks. This milk, being made with walnuts and almonds, is rich in omega-3 fatty acids. Walnuts in particular also contain arginine, a fundamental nutrient required for cell division and protein synthesis, making this a wonderful milk to serve to our growing children.

Makes about 1 quart

¾ cup walnuts
½ cup almonds
4½ cups cold water

Kosher salt
1 tablespoon maple syrup (optional)
1 teaspoon vanilla extract (optional)

1. Put the nuts in a large sealable container and add the water. Cover and put in the refrigerator overnight, or for 12 to 14 hours.

2. Drain the soaked nuts in a colander over a large bowl, reserving the soaking liquid. In a food processor or blender, blend the nuts with about half of the reserved liquid, until creamy. Add the remaining reserved liquid and blend until smooth. Pour the milk through a very fine mesh strainer placed over a large bowl, discarding the solids. Add salt to taste. If you like your milk sweetened, add the maple syrup and vanilla. Store the milk in a sealed jar in the refrigerator for up to 4 days.

vegetable stock

Keep vegetable stock on hand so you can easily boost the overall nutrient content of soups and grain dishes. When cooking rice or quinoa, for example, cook with mineral-packed stock instead of water and celebrate how much you are nourishing your family! This rich vegetable stock is unique in that it calls for red onion skins. These contain quercitin, a powerful flavonoid that acts as both an antioxidant and an anti-inflammatory. (You can use the rest of the red onions sliced in a fresh salad, or sauté and serve over quinoa; the leafy portions removed from the Swiss chard ribs can be steamed or sautéed in another dish.)

Makes about 2 quarts

Skins of 3 red onions, washed
1 large yellow onion, unpeeled, quartered
8 cloves garlic
1 large carrot, peeled and chopped
2 bunches Swiss chard, ribs only

2 stalks celery, chopped
1 sweet potato, chopped
12 sprigs fresh parsley
1 piece kombu seaweed
2½ quarts water
Sea salt, for seasoning

1. In a large soup pot, combine all the ingredients and bring to a boil. Reduce the temperature and simmer over medium-low heat, uncovered, for 30 minutes. Strain the vegetable stock through a very fine mesh strainer, discarding the solids. Use right away or store for future use. The stock keeps well in a sealed jar in the refrigerator for up to 1 week or in the freezer for up to 1 month.

Try freezing your vegetable stock in ice cube trays for handy small quantities and faster thawing. In the winter, for a powerful healing tonic, drink a cup of warm vegetable stock before breakfast. One of the interesting and unique ingredients in this vegetable stock is kombu seaweed—an outstanding source of iodine, which is essential to thyroid function and hormone production.

marinara sauce

Homemade marinara comes in handy for so many dishes. Go ahead and jar extra marinara to store in the freezer for pizza sauce on the fly, dressing rice or pasta, or dipping the Zucchini Piccata (page 133). Yes, there are nine cloves of garlic in this sauce, but the flavor becomes milder in cooking, while offering so much antibacterial and antiviral support.

Makes 9 to 10 cups

2 small red onions, finely chopped

9 cloves garlic, finely chopped

3 tablespoons extra-virgin olive oil

15 large tomatoes, diced

2 teaspoons maple syrup

1 cup fresh basil leaves, torn into small pieces or roughly chopped

¾ cup chopped fresh spinach leaves

1 tablespoon drained capers

2 tablespoons chopped fresh parsley

1 cup chopped artichoke hearts

¼ teaspoon red pepper flakes

2 teaspoons celery seeds

1½ tablespoons chopped fresh oregano

⅓ cup red wine

½ cup Vegetable Stock (page 19)

Sea salt and freshly ground black pepper

1. In a large Dutch oven over medium heat, sauté the onion and garlic in the oil until tender, 3 to 5 minutes. Stir in the tomatoes. Reduce the temperature and simmer, covered, for just under 1 minute. Stir in the maple syrup, basil, spinach, capers, parsley, artichoke hearts, red pepper flakes, celery seeds, oregano, wine, and stock. Simmer, uncovered, over low heat for 1 hour, stirring occasionally. Season to taste with salt and pepper. Use right away or store for future use. The sauce keeps well in a sealed jar in the refrigerator for up to 5 days or in the freezer for up to 1 month.

pico de gallo

My dear friend Maria swears by this Pico de Gallo recipe. It takes only a few minutes to prepare and then marinates in the refrigerator overnight. I like to serve this with the Black Bean Croquettes (page 55) or Lentil Tacos (page 117).

Makes 2¼ cups

3 medium tomatoes, seeded and diced

½ cup chopped fresh cilantro

⅓ cup very finely chopped white onion

1 small fresh serrano chile, finely chopped (or more to taste)

1 tablespoon plus 1 teaspoon freshly squeezed lime juice

¾ teaspoon sea salt

1. In a glass bowl, combine all the ingredients. Cover and refrigerate, letting the mixture marinate overnight. Drain off the excess liquid before serving, or serve with a slotted spoon. Store the pico de gallo in an airtight container in the refrigerator for up to 5 days.

breakfast

Millet Prune Porridge 25

Quinoa Porridge 26

Muesli 28

Blueberry Oat Pancakes 30

Mixed Berry Smoothie with
Chia Seeds 32

Avocado Chocolate Frappé 33

Blueberry Parsley Smoothie 34

Banana Muffins 36

Mixed Berry Muffins 38

Apple Spice Muffins 39

Carrot Muffins 40

BREAKFAST IS A SIGNIFICANT and influential meal, for children especially. After fasting all night, we all need to recharge and refuel. Having plenty of fiber and protein at breakfast produces lasting energy that sustains mental focus and the capacity to problem solve, and gives children (and adults) the physical energy to play. Breakfast is like the ignition of the body's metabolism; when the metabolism is active, it helps us to maintain a healthy weight.

The following recipes were all created with high fiber and high protein in mind. The muffins are the sweeter of the recipes (yet still much less sweet than most muffin recipes), with the exception of the Apple Spice Muffins (page 39), which are the least sweet.

millet prune porridge

Apple and prunes sweeten this creamy, warming porridge. This is my daughter's personal favorite. We always feel satisfied and ready for the day after a warm bowlful of this porridge and a glass of homemade nut milk.

Makes 3 servings

1 cup millet

3 cups water

1 small sweet-tart apple (such as Pink Lady), finely chopped

½ cup chopped prunes

1 teaspoon vanilla extract

½ teaspoon ground cinnamon

Sea salt, for seasoning

Walnut Almond Milk (page 18), for topping (optional)

½ cup lightly toasted pecans, roughly chopped, plus more for topping (optional)

1. In a medium pot, combine the millet, water, apple, prunes, vanilla, cinnamon, and salt. Bring to a boil over medium-high heat, stirring occasionally. Reduce the temperature to low and cover. Simmer until all the liquid has been absorbed and the millet is fluffy, about 20 minutes. Serve topped with milk and the pecans.

quinoa porridge

If you want to start the day with a high-protein porridge, look no further. Not only is quinoa high in protein, but it is a complete protein, which is very rare for a grain. Don't be daunted by all the ingredients; this porridge comes together quickly. The orange zest is optional, but I urge you to try it; the splash of citrus goes well with the cinnamon and berries. In my family, two of us love shredded coconut, another not so much—so we offer it in a serving bowl.

Makes 4 servings

1¼ cups quinoa
½ teaspoon ground cinnamon
3 cups Walnut Almond Milk (page 18), plus more for serving
2 tablespoons maple syrup
1 teaspoon vanilla extract
½ teaspoon almond extract

½ teaspoon freshly grated orange zest (optional)
Sea salt, for seasoning
2 cups fresh mixed berries
½ cup lightly toasted pecans, roughly chopped
¼ cup unsweetened shredded coconut, lightly toasted (optional)

1. In a medium pot, combine the quinoa, cinnamon, milk, maple syrup, vanilla, almond extract, orange zest, and salt. Bring to a boil over medium-high heat, stirring occasionally. Reduce the temperature to low and cover. Cook until all the liquid has been absorbed, about 15 minutes.

2. Stir the porridge briefly. Divide the porridge among 4 bowls, and top each with ½ cup of the berries and a sprinkling of the pecans and coconut. Add additional milk for serving.

muesli

This cereal is filled with whole food goodness, and there is certainly an abundance of fiber! I love the variety of seeds and nuts, with their rich, healthy oils—plus, pumpkin seeds supply zinc, Brazil nuts are exceptionally high in selenium and B-complex vitamins, and walnuts are a great source of vitamin E.

Makes fourteen ½-cup servings

1 cup almonds, chopped
1 cup unsweetened shredded
   coconut
2 cups gluten-free rolled oats
½ cup sunflower seeds
½ cup pumpkin seeds
½ cup raisins

½ cup pitted chopped dates
¼ cup dried goji berries
½ cup Brazil nuts, chopped
¼ cup walnuts, chopped
Walnut Almond Milk (page 18),
   or Nut Milk Yogurt (page 10),
   for topping

1. In a large mixing bowl, combine the almonds, coconut, oats, sunflower seeds, pumpkin seeds, raisins, dates, berries, Brazil nuts, and walnuts. Transfer the mixture to a large airtight container and store in the refrigerator for up to 1 month. To serve, top with milk.

Oats, as we know, are such a nutritious and satisfying food. They are also good for our skin, when used topically. At our house we take oat baths regularly! Oats applied externally, such as in a bath, or cooked and applied like a mud mask, simultaneously soothe the skin and protect it from irritants. A tepid oat bath really does wonders to relieve sunburn and itchy skin (even from poison ivy, poison oak, and other itchy rashes). The fats in the oats lubricate the skin, alleviating dryness, and the proteins create a creamy film that acts as a barricade, inhibiting histamines and inflammatory compounds from getting through to the skin. Oats are helpful in healing wounds too. They assist in cleaning out bacteria while providing nutrients to promote healing.

Making an oat bath is simple. Fill a sock two-thirds full with rolled oats, and tie a strong knot to secure the top. Put the oat-filled sock in your tub and fill up the bath. While in the tub, continue squeezing the oat-filled sock. Soon your tub will be filled with creamy, soothing oat milk!

blueberry oat pancakes

Having pancakes for breakfast can feel like such an indulgence. This recipe, full of oats, flax, and blueberries, provides a breakfast that fuels the body with lasting energy. For our family, they've become a weekend tradition. While they are already rich with berries in the batter, I recommend topping them with extra fresh blueberries. To really go all out, serve with coconut cream and a drizzle of maple syrup.

Makes ten 4-inch pancakes

1½ cups water

¼ cup flax meal

2 tablespoons maple syrup, plus
   more for serving (optional)

1 teaspoon vanilla extract

2 tablespoons canola oil

2 cups gluten-free quick oats,
   pulverized in a food processor,
   or 2 cups oat flour

½ teaspoon baking soda

½ teaspoon baking powder

1 teaspoon ground cinnamon

¼ teaspoon kosher salt

1 cup fresh or frozen blueberries,
   plus more for serving (optional)

2 tablespoons coconut oil,
   for cooking

Coconut cream, for serving
   (optional)

1. In a large mixing bowl, combine the water, flax meal, maple syrup, vanilla, and canola oil. Let stand for 10 minutes. Meanwhile, in a medium mixing bowl, combine the oats, baking soda, baking powder, cinnamon, and salt. Combine the wet ingredients with the dry ingredients. Gently fold in the blueberries.

2. Heat a large griddle (I like to use a cast-iron griddle) over medium-high heat. Lightly coat the griddle with coconut oil. Drop ¼-cup portions of batter onto the griddle. Cook until little bubbles rise to the surface. Flip the pancakes and cook on the other side for about 1½ minutes; transfer to serving plates. Continue until all the batter has been cooked. Serve with coconut cream, blueberries, and maple syrup.

mixed berry smoothie
with chia seeds

This smoothie is robust, with berries full of antioxidants, chlorophyll-rich greens, and high-protein chia seeds. Chia seeds are actually a complete protein and an excellent source of omega-3 and omega-6 fatty acids, and calcium (one 3-tablespoon serving contains 233 milligrams). For a thicker smoothie with more sweetness, add one small banana—the potassium boost can also help ease young children's growing pains.

Makes 1 to 2 servings

1½ cups Walnut Almond Milk
   (page 18)
½ cup frozen blueberries
½ cup frozen blackberries

1 cup fresh spinach
½ cup pitted chopped dates
1½ tablespoons chia seeds

1. In a blender, combine all the ingredients and process on high speed until very creamy. Divide into glasses and serve.

avocado chocolate frappé

This rich, icy frappé is just the kind of treat I love to blend up for my daughter, Lilli. It is as rich as an ice cream shake but full of nutrients, healthy fats, and even protein! Did you know that avocados contain eighteen amino acids (including all the essential ones) to form a complete protein? The protein is very easy to absorb due to avocado's high fiber content. Avocados also handsomely provide many phytonutrients, thus delivering high-quality vitamin A to our bodies. If, like me, you prefer less sweetness, try using less maple syrup—start with a tablespoon and taste; add more if you like.

Makes 2 servings

½ ripe medium avocado
¼ cup maple syrup
1½ cups Walnut Almond Milk
   (page 18)

3 tablespoons cocoa powder
¼ teaspoon ground cinnamon
8 ice cubes

1. In a blender, combine all the ingredients and process on high speed until very creamy. Divide into glasses and serve.

> For adults who like coffee, add 2 shots espresso or ½ cup strongly brewed coffee to the blender per serving. Or, when making this to share with a youngster, make the frappé without the coffee first. Pour their serving into a glass and blend the rest with the espresso or coffee. This is my favorite afternoon treat for boosting brain activity and energy so I can be more fun at the playground with my daughter!

blueberry parsley smoothie

What a gift to give your taste buds and body! Packed with blueberries, kale, and parsley, this smoothie delivers a wealth of vitamin K, vitamin C, antioxidants, and fiber. The powerful parsley adds a refreshing note, balanced by the sweetness of the banana and dates. Make this bone-building smoothie often and rejoice in nourishing your family!

Makes 1 to 2 servings

1 cup Walnut Almond Milk (page 18) or water
1 cup frozen blueberries
1 banana

1½ cups stemmed torn kale leaves
½ cup chopped fresh parsley
½ cup pitted chopped dates

1. Combine all the ingredients in a blender and process on high speed until very creamy. Divide into glasses and serve.

banana muffins

The flours, oats, flax, and pecans in these muffins deliver protein, quality fat, and high fiber, which all contribute to lasting energy. And the muffins feature maple syrup, which is my favorite sweetener because it is so rich in minerals—including manganese, zinc, and more calcium than any other sweetener. If you are feeling decadent and want to turn this breakfast muffin into a dessert or treat muffin, add one-half to three-quarters cup of chopped dark chocolate—and enjoy one while they're still warm.

Makes 12 muffins

2 tablespoons flax meal
⅔ cup water
1½ cups mashed very ripe bananas
   (about 3 medium bananas)
½ cup maple syrup
½ cup canola oil or melted
   coconut oil
2 teaspoons freshly squeezed
   lemon juice

1 teaspoon vanilla extract
1¼ cups brown rice flour
½ cup gluten-free oat, teff,
   or millet flour
½ teaspoon baking powder
¾ teaspoon baking soda
½ teaspoon sea salt
¾ cup chopped pecans

1. In a small bowl, combine the flax meal and water and set in the refrigerator to thicken, about 10 to 15 minutes.

2. Set an oven rack in the middle of the oven. Preheat the oven to 375 degrees F. Line a 12-cup standard muffin tin with cupcake liners.

3. In a large mixing bowl, combine the bananas with the maple syrup, oil, lemon juice, and vanilla. In a medium mixing bowl, combine the brown rice flour, oat flour, baking powder, baking soda, and salt. Add the flax-meal mixture to the wet ingredients. Fold the dry ingredients into the wet ingredients

until just incorporated, being careful not to overmix. Fill each muffin cup two-thirds full. Top each with 1 tablespoon of the pecans.

4. Bake on the middle rack of the oven until the tops are golden and spring back when touched, or when a toothpick inserted in the center comes out with just a few crumbs attached, about 20 to 25 minutes. Let the muffins rest in their baking cups for 5 minutes before transferring to a rack to cool. Cool muffins completely before storing in an airtight container. The muffins can be stored for up to 3 days in the refrigerator or up to 1 month in the freezer.

The flax meal in this recipe acts as a binder, much as eggs would. If you have any non-vegan recipes calling for eggs that you'd now like to make vegan, you can replace the eggs with a flax-meal mixture. For each egg you are replacing, grind 1 tablespoon of raw flaxseeds to a fine grind. In a medium bowl, combine the ground flaxseeds with 3 tablespoons of cold water for each tablespoon of flaxseed. Whisk thoroughly and refrigerate for 10 to 15 minutes to thicken. Proceed with your recipe, adding the flax-meal mixture where the eggs are called for. This replacement works best for cookies, muffins, and brownies. Chia seeds with water make another excellent egg substitute. Follow the same steps; however, the chia seed mixture needs to chill for only 5 minutes.

mixed berry muffins

These high-fiber muffins get a nutritional boost from gluten-free oat flour. Notable for both iron and protein, oats can also enhance the immune system's response to bacterial infections. It's the beta-glucan in oats that helps immune cells find infections quickly as well as vanquish the bacteria, which speeds healing. Oats also help stabilize blood sugar. Such a helpful tool to have in our kitchen "medicine cabinet"!

Makes 12 muffins

½ cup canola oil

½ cup maple syrup

¾ cup Walnut Almond Milk (page 18)

2 teaspoons apple cider vinegar

1 teaspoon vanilla extract

1¼ cups gluten-free oat flour

½ cup millet flour

¾ teaspoon baking powder

½ teaspoon baking soda

½ teaspoon sea salt

¾ teaspoon ground cinnamon

1¼ cup fresh or frozen mixed
   berries, divided

1. Set an oven rack in the middle of the oven. Preheat the oven to 375 degrees F. Line a 12-cup standard muffin tin with cupcake liners.

2. In a large mixing bowl, combine the oil, maple syrup, milk, vinegar, and vanilla. In a medium mixing bowl, combine the oat flour, millet flour, baking powder, baking soda, salt, and cinnamon. Fold the dry ingredients into the wet ingredients until just incorporated, being careful not to overmix. Fold in ¾ cup of the berries. Fill each muffin cup two-thirds full. Equally distribute the remaining ½ cup berries over the top of each muffin.

3. Bake on the middle rack of the oven until the tops are golden and spring back when touched, or when a toothpick inserted in the center comes out with just a few crumbs attached, about 20 to 25 minutes. Let the muffins rest in their baking cups for 5 minutes before transferring to a rack to cool. Cool muffins completely before storing in an airtight container. The muffins can be stored for up to 3 days in the refrigerator or up to 1 month in the freezer.

apple spice muffins

These muffins really shine because of the minimal amount of sweetener and very high fiber content. They are yummiest when eaten warm—especially when spread with a smidgen of coconut oil.

Makes 10 muffins

½ cup canola oil
1 cup water
¼ cup molasses
½ cup flax meal
1 teaspoon vanilla extract
1¼ cups teff flour
½ teaspoon ground cinnamon

½ teaspoon baking soda
½ teaspoon baking powder
¼ teaspoon kosher salt
½ cup unsweetened shredded coconut
1 apple, grated with the peel (about ¾ cup)

1. Set an oven rack in the middle of the oven. Preheat the oven to 375 degrees F. Line a 12-cup standard muffin tin with 10 cupcake liners.

2. In a large mixing bowl, combine the oil, water, molasses, flax meal, and vanilla. In a medium mixing bowl, combine the flour, cinnamon, baking soda, baking powder, and salt. Fold the dry ingredients into the wet ingredients until just incorporated, being careful not to overmix. Fold in the coconut and apple. Fill each muffin cup one-half full.

3. Bake on the middle rack of the oven until the tops are golden and spring back when touched, or when a toothpick inserted in the center comes out with just a few crumbs attached, about 20 to 25 minutes. Let the muffins rest in their baking cups for 5 minutes before transferring to a rack to cool. Cool muffins completely before storing in an airtight container. The muffins can be stored for up to 3 days in the refrigerator; their density and fragility do not make for good long-term storage in the freezer.

carrot muffins

I love these muffins so much, I had them for dessert with my family on my birthday! They are full of gloriously health-promoting ingredients, with lots of fiber and beta carotene from the carrots and apricots. They are delicately sweet and full of flavor from the baking spices, plump raisins, and apricots, along with bursts of nutty pecan sweetness.

Makes 12 muffins

½ cup flax meal

⅓ cup plus 2 tablespoons applesauce

½ cup coconut milk

⅓ cup maple syrup

⅓ cup canola oil

½ cup brown rice flour

½ cup millet flour

½ cup almond meal

1 cup chopped pecans

2¼ teaspoons ground cinnamon

½ teaspoon ground nutmeg

¼ teaspoon ground ginger

1 teaspoon baking soda

1 teaspoon baking powder

½ teaspoon sea salt

1 cup peeled grated carrot

1 tablespoon grated orange peel

⅓ cup raisins

⅓ cup chopped dried apricots

1. Set an oven rack in the middle of the oven. Preheat the oven to 375 degrees F. Line a 12-cup standard muffin tin with cupcake liners.

2. In a medium mixing bowl, combine the flax meal, applesauce, milk, maple syrup, and oil.

3. In a large mixing bowl, combine the brown rice flour, millet flour, almond meal, pecans, cinnamon, nutmeg, ginger, baking soda, baking powder, and salt. Stir in the carrot, orange peel, raisins, and apricot, until just incorporated, being careful not to overmix. Add the flax meal mixture to the carrot mixture and stir to incorporate all the ingredients. Fill each muffin cup two-thirds full.

4. Bake on the middle rack of the oven until the tops are golden and spring back when touched, or when a toothpick inserted in the center comes out with just a few crumbs attached, about 35 minutes. Let the muffins rest in their baking cups for about 5 minutes before transferring to a rack to cool. Cool muffins completely before storing in an airtight container. The muffins can be stored for up to 3 days in the refrigerator or up to 1 month in the freezer.

lunch

Red Bean Burgers 45

Chickpea Salad Sandwich 48

TLT Sandwich 49

Open-Face Cucumber Cream
Cheese Sandwich 51

Soba Noodle Summer Rolls 53

Black Bean Croquettes 55

Chickpea Croquettes 56

Samosas 57

Red Bean and Rice
Mini Cakes 59

Spring Rolls with Chickpeas 60

Lentil Caviar on Root
Vegetable Rounds 62

Herbed Soft Cheese and
Tomato Sandwich 65

Quinoa Tabbouleh 66

Caponata 68

IN THE MIDDLE OF THE DAY, after we've used up our breakfast fuel, having lunch re-energizes us, raises our blood sugar level (creating better moods in kids especially!), and keeps our metabolism performing well.

For adults, taking a lunch break and getting outdoors refreshes the mind for a more creative and productive afternoon. Eating while continuing to work can increase stress and therefore increase cortisol production, which has many downsides, including accretion of fat. So take some well-deserved time off to recharge in the company of friends over a healthy, satisfying meal. And for a true break in the middle of a busy day, simple recipes fit the bill.

I've noticed that when it comes to lunch, many of us get into a rut, especially in what we pack to eat away from home. For packed lunches, consider the Red Bean and Rice Mini Cakes (page 59). They can be made the night before, reheated in the morning, and packed in a thermos to keep them warm. All the sandwiches also pack up with ease, and if you don't have the time to make your own cheese, you can go with store-bought vegan options.

Some of the lunch recipes, such as the Lentil Caviar on Root Vegetable Rounds (page 62), are meant for a fancy lunch party and wouldn't travel as well.

red bean burgers

With this burger, full of red beans and quinoa, you are serving a capital source of protein, iron, and fiber. When choosing delicious condiments to go with your burger, there are a lot of nice choices, but one ingredient to avoid is high-fructose corn syrup. Thankfully, there are now quite a few ketchups made with all-natural ingredients. I really like the taste of Annie's brand ketchup, and the ingredients are simple and few. Serve these burgers on the Sandwich Bread (page 7) made into buns!

Makes 4 to 6 patties

½ cup rainbow quinoa, rinsed

1 tablespoon plus 1 teaspoon canola oil, divided, plus more for oiling

1 cup water

Sea salt, for seasoning

1 medium yam, peeled and diced

1 red onion, diced

2 cloves garlic, minced

½ teaspoon cumin

1 tablespoon chile powder

¼ cup fresh cilantro, loosely packed and finely chopped

1½ cups cooked small red beans, or 1 (15-ounce) can, rinsed and drained

4 to 6 buns

Ketchup (optional)

Grain mustard (optional)

1 avocado, sliced

4 to 6 slices large heirloom or beefsteak tomatoes

4 to 6 lettuce leaves

½ red onion, thinly sliced

1. In a medium pot, combine the quinoa, 1 teaspoon of the oil, the water, and salt over high heat and bring to a boil. Reduce the temperature to low and cook, covered, until the water has been absorbed and the quinoa is fluffy, about 15 minutes.

(continued)

2. While the quinoa cooks, in a steaming basket, steam the yam until tender, about 10 minutes. Transfer to a mixing bowl and mash with a fork or potato masher.

3. Preheat the oven to 375 degrees F. In a medium pan, heat the remaining 1 tablespoon oil over medium heat and sauté the onion, garlic, cumin, chile powder, and cilantro until the spices are fragrant and the onion has softened, about 3 to 4 minutes. Lightly oil a baking sheet.

4. Add the quinoa, beans, and sautéed onion mixture to the yam. Stir and mash slightly until everything holds together. With your hands, form patties into equal portions, making 4 large patties or 6 medium patties. Put the patties on the baking sheet and bake for 10 minutes. Flip the patties over and bake until lightly crisped on the outside, about 15 minutes more.

5. Serve the patties in buns with ketchup, mustard, avocado, tomato, lettuce, and onion.

For homemade buns to go with bean burgers, follow the recipe for Sandwich Bread (page 7) through making the dough. Preheat the oven to 375 degrees F. Generously flour a work surface with brown rice flour and line a baking sheet with parchment. Divide the dough into 8 equal portions. Gently shape the individual portions of dough into rounds, put them on the baking sheet, and flatten slightly with the palm of your hand. Using a fork, prick around the circumference of the middle of the bun. Bake until golden brown and firm to the touch, about 17 minutes. After the buns cool (about 1 hour), slice in half horizontally and assemble your burgers!

chickpea salad sandwich

The star of this show is the tasty chickpea, packed with iron, protein, and fiber. This salad is also a wonderful filler for a bun or lettuce-leaf wrap. For a time saver, make the salad the night before—the flavors intensify with the extra marinating time.

Makes 4 sandwiches

1 (15-ounce) can chickpeas, rinsed and drained
½ celery stalk, thinly sliced
1 green onion, finely chopped
⅓ cup peeled grated apple
2 tablespoons extra-virgin olive oil

1 teaspoon freshly squeezed lemon juice
½ teaspoon curry powder
½ teaspoon sea salt
8 slices Sandwich Bread (page 7)
4 Bibb lettuce leaves
1 avocado, sliced

1. In a medium bowl, mash the chickpeas with a fork so they are chunky and some are still intact. Add the celery, onion, apple, oil, lemon juice, curry powder, and salt and stir until well combined.

2. Portion the mixture onto 4 slices of the bread—I like to lightly toast my bread. Top each with lettuce, avocado, and another slice of bread.

tlt sandwich

Tempeh, a fermented soybean food, is a terrific source of protein and very easy to digest. This finger-licking-good sandwich is mouth-wateringly delicious, whether eaten chilled or still warm. If you are making it for a packed lunch, it will stay warm if you wrap it securely in parchment paper and then again with foil. If you prefer to have it chilled, you can save time in the morning rush by making the tempeh the night before and assembling the sandwich in the morning. I personally like the extra zing of Dijon mustard—if you're a fan too, try that variation. (I even dip mine in ketchup!)

Makes 4 sandwiches

2 tablespoons canola oil

2 tablespoons tamari

2 teaspoons balsamic vinegar

3 teaspoons grain mustard

2 teaspoons maple syrup

1 teaspoon chile powder

16 ounces tempeh

8 slices Sandwich Bread (page 7)

1 avocado, mashed

Sea salt and freshly ground
   black pepper

Vegan mayonnaise (optional)

Dijon mustard (optional)

4 slices large heirloom
   or beefsteak tomato

2 cups micro greens

1. In a small bowl, whisk together the oil, tamari, vinegar, mustard, maple syrup, and chile powder. Slice the tempeh into squares roughly the size of the sandwich bread. Make each square thinner by carefully slicing through the center. Arrange the tempeh in a single layer in a large glass baking dish. Pour the marinade over the tempeh, coating each piece. Marinate the tempeh for 15 minutes and then flip, marinating for 15 minutes more. Preheat the oven to 375 degrees F.

(continued)

2. Bake the tempeh until golden and browned, about 20 to 25 minutes.

3. Lightly toast the bread. Season the avocado with salt and pepper to taste. Spread the avocado on half of the slices of bread and mayonnaise and mustard on the other half of the slices of bread. Build the sandwiches according to your preference—I like my tempeh between the tomato and greens—and serve.

open-face cucumber
cream cheese sandwich

For a tea party, this sandwich fits the bill! If you want to prepare it in the English style, slice the bread into bite-size squares and build little open-face sandwiches with a spread of the cream cheese, topped with a very thin slice of cucumber. Arrange on a tiered or cake pedestal.

Makes 8 sandwiches

1 English cucumber, one-half peeled and cut into ⅛-inch dice, one-half sliced into 8 thin rounds
½ cup mint leaves, julienned

2 cups Cream Cheese (page 14), at room temperature
Sea salt and freshly ground black pepper
8 slices Sandwich Bread (page 7)

1. In a medium bowl, fold the diced cucumber and mint into the cream cheese, and season to taste with salt and pepper.

2. Spread a generous ¼ cup of the cream cheese mixture onto each slice of bread. Top with the cucumber rounds and serve.

> One of the quickest to make and most common sandwiches for a packed lunch is, of course, good old-fashioned peanut butter and jelly. In a pinch, thick slices of sandwich bread slathered with a favorite nut butter (like cashew, almond, walnut, or sunflower seed) and smashed sweet blackberries taste amazing!

soba noodle summer rolls

There is so much goodness in these mouthwatering summer rolls—bright antioxidant-rich vegetables, creamy avocado loaded with vitamin E, powerful immune-supporting shiitake mushrooms, protein-rich tofu, and satisfying buckwheat noodles! The rice paper wrappers are very sticky, so they hold the rolls together beautifully.

Makes 12 rolls

10 shiitake mushrooms, stemmed
    and thinly sliced

⅓ cup tamari

3 ounces 100 percent buckwheat
    soba noodles

½ cup sesame seeds

12 rice paper wrappers

14 ounces tofu, cut into
    thin rectangles

1 small cucumber, peeled and
    thinly sliced

1 medium carrot,
    peeled and julienned

½ avocado, cut into thin slices

1 cup fresh basil leaves, finely
    chopped

1 cup fresh cilantro leaves,
    finely chopped

½ small red onion, minced
    (about ½ cup)

2 teaspoons chile oil

1 cup rice wine vinegar

1 green onion, minced

1. In a small bowl, combine the mushrooms and tamari to marinate.

2. Bring a medium pot of water to a boil and then reduce the heat to a simmer. Cook the noodles for 8 minutes. Drain and rinse the noodles under cold water. Slice the noodles into 2-inch lengths.

(continued)

3. In a dry skillet over medium heat, roast the sesame seeds until they brown slightly and smell fragrant.

4. Prepare a large container of cold water to soften the rice paper wrappers. (I use a large sauté pan because the size and shallow depth work well.) Assembling 1 roll at a time, lay 1 paper in the water until softened, about 2 to 3 minutes. Put the softened wrapper on a flat surface and arrange the mushrooms, noodles, tofu, cucumber, carrots, avocado, basil, cilantro, onion, and the sesame seeds in a line down the center of the wrapper. Sprinkle with oil and, working with your hands, lift up the edge of the rice paper below the filling and fold it over the filling toward the center. Next, fold in the sides of the rice paper toward each other. Finally, roll up the roll. Continue in this way with the remaining filling and rice papers.

5. To make the dipping sauce, in a small bowl, combine the vinegar and green onion. Slice each roll in half to expose the vibrant colors of the filling. Serve with the dipping sauce on the side.

> Softened rice paper wrappers are very sticky, so to keep the rolls from sticking to one another in a packed lunch, wrap a bit of parchment paper around each before packing snugly in a container.

black bean croquettes

In these tasty croquettes, the bread crumbs combined with the beans provide a superb complete protein, plus high fiber to keep you energized for several hours! I've noticed too, that when little ones take out their packed lunches, they usually eat more of the finger foods like these than the dishes that require a utensil. Because the croquettes are best served warm, sometimes I pack them in my daughter's thermos.

Makes 8 croquettes

1½ cups cooked black beans,
    or 1 (15-ounce) can, rinsed
    and drained
1 large sweet potato, peeled, diced,
    and steamed until softened
¼ cup very finely chopped onion
1 clove garlic
2½ tablespoons minced fresh parsley

1 teaspoon sea salt
½ teaspoon ground cumin
½ teaspoon freshly ground
    black pepper
1½ cups gluten-free bread crumbs
¼ cup canola oil
1 avocado, sliced, for serving
Salsa, for serving

1. In a food processor, combine the beans, sweet potato, onion, garlic, parsley, salt, cumin, and pepper. Process just until the ingredients hold together and the mixture is still a little bit chunky. Cover a plate with the bread crumbs. Divide the bean mixture into 8 equal-size balls, and with slightly dampened hands, form into patties. Generously coat each patty with crumbs and put on a baking sheet. Refrigerate the formed croquettes for 30 minutes before cooking.

2. In a skillet over medium heat, heat the oil. Cook the croquettes for 3½ to 4 minutes on each side and serve hot alongside avocado and salsa.

chickpea croquettes

Chickpeas mixed with bread crumbs create a complete protein. There's just enough onion in these croquettes to add flavor but still be mild enough for a child's taste buds. Including onions in the diet regularly is proven to increase bone density—try to use the outermost onion layer, as it is highest in flavonoids. You can also serve these like falafel with the Quinoa Flatbread (page 8), shredded lettuce, chopped tomato, and tahini sauce.

Makes 8 croquettes

1½ cups cooked chickpeas
  or 1 (15-ounce) can, drained
  and rinsed
1 large sweet potato, peeled, diced,
  and steamed until softened
¼ cup very finely chopped onion
¼ cup peeled grated carrot

2½ tablespoons minced fresh parsley
1 teaspoon sea salt
½ teaspoon freshly ground
  black pepper
1 cup gluten-free bread crumbs
¼ cup canola oil
Chutney, for serving

1. In a food processor, combine the chickpeas, sweet potato, onion, carrot, parsley, salt, and pepper. Process just until the ingredients hold together and the mixture is still a little bit chunky. Cover a plate with the bread crumbs. Divide the bean mixture into 8 equal-size balls, and with slightly dampened hands, form into patties. Generously coat each patty with crumbs and put on a baking sheet. Refrigerate the formed croquettes for 30 minutes before cooking.

2. In a skillet over medium heat, heat the oil. Cook the croquettes for 3½ to 4 minutes on each side and serve hot with the chutney.

samosas

These samosas are unique in that the pastry surrounding the filling contains protein from the chickpea flour, almonds, and flaxseeds. Try making these with the Dhal Soup (page 83) and Pakoras (page 97) for a splendid Indian meal. My favorite chutney to serve with the pakoras and samosas is Organic Date & Tamarind Chutney by Vedica Organics. It can be ordered from Amazon and is also sold at specialty grocery stores. If you have the desire and the time, try making some of your own chutneys! You can better control the spice level this way too. One glimpse of all the possibilities for exotic chutneys will leave your mouth watering.

Makes 32 samosas

1½ packages rapid rise yeast

2¼ cups warm water

3 cups chickpea flour

3 cups almond meal

1½ cups flax meal

3½ teaspoons sea salt, divided

3 tablespoons coconut oil,
   melted, divided, plus more
   for oiling

1 teaspoon cumin seeds

1 teaspoon mustard seeds

1 tablespoon curry powder

¼ teaspoon cayenne (optional)

2 small yellow onions, minced

4 cloves garlic

2 large sweet potatoes, baked,
   skins removed

1 cup fresh or frozen green peas

Brown rice flour, for dusting

1. To make the dough, in a small bowl, dissolve the yeast in the water and let stand for 10 minutes. In a large mixing bowl, combine the chickpea flour, almond meal flour, flax meal, 3 teaspoons of the salt, and 1 tablespoon of the oil. Add the yeast and water mixture. Transfer the mixture to the bowl of a stand mixer fitted with the dough hook attachment (or to a bowl to mix by

(continued)

hand) and mix until a ball of dough forms, about 7 minutes. Cover and set aside in a warm place to rise for 1 hour.

2. While the dough is rising, make the samosa filling. In a large skillet, dry roast the cumin and mustard seeds just until they become fragrant and begin to pop. Set aside on a plate. In the same skillet, heat 1 tablespoon of the oil with the curry and cayenne over medium-low heat. Sauté the spices for a moment to further release their flavors. Add the onion and garlic and cook until softened, about 5 minutes. Add the seed mixture, sweet potato, and peas. Cook, stirring, for 7 to 8 minutes, sprinkling in the remaining ½ teaspoon salt.

3. Preheat the oven to 375 degrees F and lightly oil a baking sheet. Generously dust a work surface with brown rice flour. Divide the dough in half and roll the halves into two 16-inch squares about ⅛ inch thick. Cut each square into sixteen 4-inch squares, creating 32 squares total. Place a rounded tablespoon of the filling in the center of each square. Fold one corner of the dough over to meet the diagonally opposite other corner, creating a triangle. With the tines of a fork, seal the edges closed. With a spatula, transfer the samosas to the baking sheet. Brush the samosas with the remaining 1 tablespoon oil. Bake until lightly browned, about 20 minutes, and serve hot.

red bean and rice mini cakes

These little cakes are another high-protein, high-fiber lunch option. The forbidden rice is a special and unique heirloom rice. It is deep purple and a good source of iron, magnesium, molybdenum, and phosphorus. The well-known Dr. Oz recommends forbidden rice as a remedy for fighting fatigue. Combined with the most powerful antioxidant food of all (the small red bean), this makes for an invigorating and healthful meal! And these little mini cakes are versatile—fantastic on their own or with a dab of guacamole or even a vegan aioli.

Makes 24 cakes

2½ tablespoons canola oil, divided
1 medium red onion, finely chopped
1 small red bell pepper, seeded and finely chopped
1 shallot, finely chopped
2 cloves garlic, finely chopped
¾ teaspoon sweet paprika
½ teaspoon dried thyme

Sea salt and freshly ground black pepper
1½ cups cooked small red beans (not adzuki), or 1 (15-ounce) can, rinsed and drained
½ cup cooked forbidden rice
3 tablespoons chopped fresh parsley
½ cup almond meal

1. In a large skillet, heat 1 tablespoon of the oil and sauté the onion, bell pepper, shallot, garlic, paprika, and thyme until the vegetables have softened, about 7 minutes. Season to taste with salt and pepper and set aside.

2. Combine the beans, rice, and parsley in a food processor and pulse 4 to 5 times, keeping some of the beans intact. Shape the mixture into golf ball–size balls and flatten each into a patty. Put the almond meal on a plate. In a large skillet over medium heat, heat the remaining 1½ tablespoons oil. Dip each patty in the almond meal and sauté for about 5 minutes on each side. Serve hot.

spring rolls with chickpeas

These spring rolls, with a lively citrus dipping sauce, make a superb appetizer or a satisfying and cooling lunch. High-protein chickpeas are an unusual addition, and the rolls are also chock-full of vibrant, antioxidant-rich vegetables and fresh herbs—the basil stands out in bright bursts of flavor.

Makes 8 rolls

Juice of 1 lime
Juice of 1 small orange
½ teaspoon minced peeled
    fresh ginger
1 small clove garlic, minced
½ cup tamari
¼ cup water
¼ head purple cabbage,
    finely julienned
½ bunch fresh cilantro,
    roughly chopped
4 scallions, thinly sliced diagonally

8 fresh basil leaves, thinly sliced
    (chiffonade)
10 mint leaves, chopped
1 small carrot, peeled and grated
1 red bell pepper, seeded
    and julienned
1 cup cooked chickpeas, or 1 cup
    from 1 (15-ounce can), rinsed
    and drained
8 rice paper wrappers
1 large avocado, sliced into
    16 thin slices

1. To make the dipping sauce, in a small bowl, whisk the juices, ginger, garlic, tamari, and water to combine. Set aside.

2. To make the spring rolls, in a medium bowl combine the cabbage, cilantro, scallions, basil, mint, carrot, bell pepper, and chickpeas.

3. Prepare a large container of cold water to soften the rice paper wrappers. (I use a large sauté pan because the size and shallow depth work well.) Assembling 1 roll at a time, lay 1 paper in the water until softened, about 2 to 3 minutes. Put the softened wrapper on a flat surface and measure ½ cup of the chickpea mixture. Place the filling just below the center of the circle of paper. Place two thin slices of avocado on top. Working with your hands, lift up the edge of the rice paper below the filling and fold it over the filling toward the center. Next, fold in the sides of the rice paper toward each other. Finally, roll up the roll. Continue in this way with the remaining filling and rice papers. Serve with the dipping sauce.

lentil caviar on
root vegetable rounds

This delectable dish is suitable for a fancy luncheon or as an appetizer for a dinner party. The lentil topping, with its intriguing flavors of seaweed and green tea, can be made in advance and reheated before topping the root vegetable rounds, which taste best when served fresh. I like the bright contrast of a parsley garnish.

Makes 4 servings

2 large yams

1 large beet

5 tablespoons canola oil

Sea salt

½ cup French green lentils or black beluga lentils

1½ cups water

2 tablespoons extra-virgin olive oil

1 medium shallot, minced

¼ cup arame seaweed

½ cup brewed green tea

2 teaspoons maple syrup

⅛ cup capers

Fresh flat leaf parsley, finely chopped, for garnish (optional)

1. To prepare the vegetable rounds, preheat the oven to 400 degrees F. Carefully slice the yams and beets very thinly, about ⅛ inch thick. A mandoline or a very sharp knife will do the trick. In a mixing bowl, toss the vegetables with the canola oil to coat. Arrange the beet and yam slices on a baking sheet in a single layer. Season the slices with salt and bake for 7 minutes. Flip the rounds and bake for 7 minutes more, until crisp and lightly browned. Transfer the rounds to wire racks to cool.

2. To make the "caviar," in a medium pot, combine the lentils with the water and bring to a boil. Reduce to a low simmer and cover. Cook until most of the water has been absorbed and the lentils are tender, about 20 minutes. Drain the lentils and set aside in a medium bowl.

3. In a large sauté pan, heat the olive oil and sauté the shallot and arame until crisp, about 4 minutes. Stir in the green tea and maple syrup and continue cooking until the liquid has reduced to a light syrup, about 6 minutes more.

4. Add the shallot mixture to the lentils and toss well. To serve, place a spoonful of the "caviar" atop each vegetable round. Garnish with the capers and parsley and serve.

herbed soft cheese and tomato sandwich

This is a terrific sandwich for nurturing strong bones and teeth, as almonds are super sources of calcium, magnesium, and phosphorus. The herbed soft cheese is full of protein, and so is the sandwich bread! And I always approve of a meal that contains something fermented; here the herbed cheese provides that healthy bacteria. This is an easy sandwich to pack, as it whips up in no time. Try serving it with the Sweet Potato and Beet Chips (page 76).

Makes 4 sandwiches

8 slices Sandwich Bread (page 7)
1 cup mixed baby greens
4 large Roma tomatoes, cut
   into slices
Extra-virgin olive oil, for drizzling

1 avocado, cut into 16 wedges
Kosher salt and freshly ground
   black pepper
Herbed Soft Cheese (page 12)

1. Top 4 slices of the bread with the greens. Place slices of the tomato on top of the greens and drizzle with oil, followed by the avocado. Season to taste with salt and pepper. Depending on how soft the cheese is, either spread it thickly on the remaining 4 slices of bread, or slice rounds of cheese and place on top of the avocado. Finally, place the cheese-smeared slices on the prepared sandwich halves. Cut each sandwich in half diagonally and serve.

> On a hot day, consider wrapping your sandwiches up with a lettuce leaf instead of bread. This lighter and refreshing method works well with the Herbed Soft Cheese and Tomato Sandwich, the Chickpea Salad Sandwich (page 48), and the TLT Sandwich (page 49). For a time saver, make your sandwich fillings the night before.

quinoa tabbouleh

Tabbouleh is an easy go-to recipe for potlucks, picnics, and packed lunches. Traditional tabbouleh is made with couscous, but one day someone discovered that quinoa makes a fabulous substitute. Quinoa adds protein, and so do the tasty white beans.

Makes 4 to 6 servings

2 cups cooked red quinoa

2 tablespoons extra-virgin olive oil

2 cloves garlic, finely chopped

Juice of 1 lemon

2 Roma tomatoes, diced

1 small cucumber, diced

1 cup cooked white beans,
    or 1 cup from 1 (15-ounce) can,
    rinsed and drained

½ small red onion, diced

1 cup chopped fresh flat leaf parsley

2 tablespoons chopped fresh mint

Sea salt and freshly ground
    black pepper

1. In a large nonreactive bowl, combine all the ingredients well and season to taste with salt and pepper. Chill for at least 1 hour before serving to allow the flavors to meld.

The red quinoa is visually exquisite in this recipe, and the white beans stand out in contrast to the reddish-brown, lacy grains. Red quinoa has a nuttier and slightly more pungent taste; I love it, but younger children tend to prefer white quinoa's mellower flavor. Unless your quinoa is prerinsed or sprouted, be sure to rinse it before cooking. This removes a bitter-tasting coating, called saponin, that protects the grain from being eaten by birds and other critters!

caponata

Caponata, generously spread over thick slices of garlic toast or the Quinoa Flatbread (page 8), makes an ideal accompaniment to a fresh salad. The primary ingredients are eggplant, tomatoes, and olives. When I serve this to children, I hold back the olives and save them for myself—a win-win for me and the kiddos (who tend to find the taste too "grown-up")! For more protein, serve this alongside the Red Bean Hummus (page 73), or a simple dish of white beans drizzled with olive oil and sprinkled with fresh herbs.

Makes 4 to 6 servings

1 medium eggplant (about 1 pound), diced

1½ tablespoons sea salt, plus more for seasoning

2 tablespoons canola oil, divided

1 small red onion, minced

2 cloves garlic, minced

6 plum tomatoes, finely chopped

½ cup pitted Niçoise olives, finely chopped

⅓ cup pine nuts, lightly toasted

2 tablespoons drained capers

¾ teaspoon red pepper flakes

¼ cup red wine vinegar

2½ tablespoons maple syrup

1 tablespoon tomato paste

½ cup roughly torn and loosely packed fresh basil leaves

Freshly ground black pepper

1. In a large bowl, put the eggplant in salted water to remove its bitter taste. Cover the eggplant with something heavy, like a small plate topped with a weight, such as a large can of beans or tomatoes, for 1 hour. Rinse the eggplant thoroughly and pat dry.

2. In a large sauté pan over medium heat, heat 1 tablespoon of the oil and sauté the onion until it begins to soften, about 4 minutes. Add the garlic and cook for 2 minutes more. Transfer to a small bowl. In the same pan over high heat, add the remaining 1 tablespoon oil and cook the eggplant for about 6 minutes, stirring every 1 to 2 minutes, to brown the eggplant on both sides.

3. Reduce the heat to medium and add the onion and garlic to the pan along with the tomatoes, olives, pine nuts, capers, and red pepper flakes, stirring with a wooden spoon to mix well. Add the vinegar, maple syrup, and tomato paste. Cook, stirring occasionally, until the eggplant is very soft, about 10 minutes. Remove from the heat and let cool to room temperature. Stir in the basil and season to taste with salt and pepper.

4. Store the caponata in a sealed container for up to 4 days in the refrigerator.

The caponata also makes an excellent pizza topping. Spread it over the tomato sauce and dot with almond feta before baking. Leftover caponata served over a bed of steamed quinoa is a welcome, quick meal to prepare at lunchtime. For a dish that is incredibly simple yet impressive when having guests over after a busy day, plan on making caponata the day before. Reheat and try serving it over bowls of piping hot polenta. This spread also goes well with bread, served along with the Heirloom Tomato Salad (page 108) and a simple green salad.

snack foods

BRINGING ALONG PACKED SNACKS when away from home can mean the difference (especially for younger children) between a delightful time and a hungry meltdown! One go-to snack that needs very little planning or preparation is a small container of nut butter and an apple. Add a paring knife (wrapped in a napkin), and you're ready to cut up the apple for dipping in the nut butter! Containers with leakproof lids are ideal for packing the Kale Chips (page 79), Nut Butter Energy Bars (page 75), and Roasted Chickpeas (page 77). The cookie recipes in Sweets and Treats (page 157) have minimal added sweeteners and make another great snack or treat for days on the go.

red bean hummus

Whenever I sense our family is getting hit with a cold bug, I like to prepare this hummus. I find the raw garlic is palatable even for young children. Hummus goes delightfully with fresh carrot sticks and lightly steamed broccoli florets, crackers, or the Quinoa Flatbread (page 8). When served with Quinoa Flatbread or crackers you are providing a complete protein, and the red beans contain absorbable iron! For a festive dinner occasion with a Middle Eastern flair, serve it alongside warm Quinoa Flatbread, topped with sumac and sliced into triangles, with a bowl of mixed olives.

Makes about 16 ounces

3 cloves garlic

1½ cups cooked small red beans, or 1 (15-ounce) can, rinsed and drained

2 tablespoons freshly squeezed lemon juice

2 teaspoons sesame oil

2 teaspoons extra-virgin olive oil

¼ teaspoon ground cumin

⅛ teaspoon smoked paprika

¼ to ½ teaspoon sea salt

Freshly ground black pepper

Fresh oregano for garnish (optional)

1. In a food processor, combine all the ingredients and blend to a smooth consistency. Store the hummus in an airtight container for up to 1 week in the refrigerator. Serve with your choice of accompaniments.

nut butter energy bars

If you feel like giving these energy bars a bit more gusto, add some finely chopped 85 percent dark chocolate—two-thirds cup will do the trick. Mix it in with the rest of the ingredients. You can also substitute goji berries for the raisins. Goji berries are unusual in that they contain all the essential amino acids and have more protein than any other fruit. They are very high in iron and also provide calcium, zinc, and selenium as well as vitamin C (which enhances iron absorption). They are a great snack food for boosting the immune system, as they contain compounds that are antifungal, antibacterial, and anti-inflammatory.

Makes 16 bars

1¼ cups nut butter (peanut butter or almond butter works best)
¾ cup maple syrup
2½ cups gluten-free rolled oats
½ cup flax meal
¼ cup sunflower seeds

¼ cup pumpkin seeds
½ cup raisins
½ teaspoon kosher salt
½ teaspoon ground cinnamon
1 teaspoon vanilla extract

1. In the bowl of a stand mixer fitted with the paddle attachment, mix all the ingredients until well combined, just under 2 minutes. Scrape down the sides of the bowl with a spatula and briefly mix again. Line a 9-by-9-inch baking pan with parchment paper. Transfer the mixture to the pan. Spread and press it smoothly with a spatula to fill the corners. Chill to set, about 1 hour. With the aid of the parchment paper, lift out the contents of the pan. Cut into 16 bars. Store in an airtight container in the refrigerator for up to 1 week.

> These bars also make a great breakfast when you're pressed for time. Prewrap the bars when you store them in the fridge so you can pop one into your bag when you're on your way out the door.

sweet potato and beet chips

These crisps don't have to be limited to sweet potatoes, yams, and beets—parsnips work well too. If your family enjoys some spice, toss them with a tablespoon of chile powder before popping them into the oven.

Makes 4 servings

Canola oil, for deep frying
1 pound yams, peeled and
    thinly sliced
1 pound red beets, peeled
    and thinly sliced

1 pound sweet potatoes, peeled
    and thinly sliced
Sea salt

1. In a large saucepan, add oil to about half full and heat to 375 degrees F. In small batches (1 cup at a time), fry the vegetable slices until crisp and slightly browned, 3 to 5 minutes. Remove the chips from the oil with a slotted spoon and put on paper towels to absorb excess oil. Season to taste with salt and serve. Cool the chips completely before storing in an airtight container for up to 3 days.

roasted chickpeas

These roasted legumes are reminiscent of spiced nuts. They are a superb and sat-isfying snack, full of protein, iron, and fiber. In this recipe, I include a fair amount of cumin, which is not only tasty but also helpful with digestion. Cumin is best when freshly ground; if you can grind your own, you'll taste the difference. If you and your family are up for some spicy heat, add the cayenne.

Makes 4 servings

2 cups cooked chickpeas, or 2 cups
    from 2 (15-ounce cans), rinsed
    and drained
3 tablespoons canola oil

1 tablespoon cumin
1 teaspoon sea salt
¼ teaspoon of cayenne (optional)

1. Preheat the oven to 400 degrees F. Lay out a clean dish towel and dry the chickpeas on it. In a medium bowl, combine the chickpeas, oil, cumin, salt, and cayenne. Transfer to a roasting pan and roast until lightly browned and crisp, about 17 minutes. Cool the chickpeas completely and store in an air-tight container for up to 3 days.

kale chips

Kale chips are the dreamiest invention for parents who struggle with getting their kids to enjoy vegetables. The texture and rich taste of these chips comes from the ground seeds in the batter that the curly kale leaves are tossed in before being baked at a very low temperature. Kale is extremely high in vitamin K, an essential nutrient for healthy, strong bones, and the pumpkin seeds, sunflower seeds, and pine nuts contribute lasting energy with excellent amino acids for tissue formation and regeneration.

Makes 4 servings

2 bunches curly green or purple kale,
   washed, dried, stemmed, and
   torn into large bite-size pieces
⅛ cup pumpkin seeds
⅛ cup sunflower seeds
¼ cup pine nuts
¼ cup water

1 tablespoon freshly squeezed
   lemon juice
1 clove garlic (optional)
3 tablespoons extra-virgin olive
   or canola oil
2 tablespoons nutritional yeast
1 teaspoon sea salt

1. Preheat the oven to its lowest setting, around 200 degrees F. Line 4 baking sheets with parchment paper. Divide the kale equally between 2 large bowls.

2. In a food processor, grind the pumpkin seeds, sunflower seeds, and pine nuts to a fine meal. Add the water, lemon juice, garlic, oil, yeast, and salt. Process all the ingredients until well incorporated.

3. Pour the batter equally over each bowl of kale. With clean hands, toss the batter and kale well.

4. Evenly distribute the kale among the baking sheets.

5. Bake until crisp but not browned, about 25 to 30 minutes. (If you don't have enough room in your oven to bake all 4 baking sheets at once, bake 2 first, and then bake the second 2.) Cool on a rack or a large plate and enjoy! Store in an airtight container for up to 3 days.

soups

SOUP IS A SUPERB ADDITION to a nutrient-rich meal. Regularly enjoying soups with a plethora of vegetables, like the ones in this chapter, helps to lower blood pressure, heart disease, and the risk of cancer as well as type 2 diabetes. They are, in general, abundant in potassium (a mineral that counters sodium intake), vitamin A (crucial for healthy eyes as well as immune action), riboflavin (for red blood cell production), and fiber. And vegetables cooked in stock retain much more of these nutrients than those cooked by sautéing or other methods.

Soups are a joy to make and don't require much fuss. I love making a big pot that serves as dinner that night and lunch for the next day. They are also easy to ladle into a thermos for a packed lunch. For a complete protein, serve these soups with the Quinoa Flatbread (page 8) and dipping oil, and perhaps the Red Bean Hummus (page 73). You can also serve these soups with a side of vegetables to make a very fine supper. The Cauliflower Bisque (page 86), for example, pairs terrifically with the Purple Potato Niçoise-Style Salad (page 111), as does the Carrot Ginger Bisque (page 84) with the Bok Choy with Seeds (page 100).

dhal soup

This soup, thick with lentils, provides sustaining energy. Lentils are digested slowly and are full of fiber. I also love the abundant, leafy spinach greens. The Indian dhal spices are not only flavorful but also full of nutrients: mustard seeds are high in selenium, and ginger is warming and helps with circulation. Try serving this soup with the Pakoras (page 97) or Samosas (page 57).

Makes 4 servings

3 tablespoons canola oil, divided
1 tablespoon mustard seeds
2 teaspoons coriander seeds
1 teaspoon dried turmeric
1 teaspoon cumin seeds
½ teaspoon fennel seeds
1 medium yellow onion, diced
   (about 1 cup)
1 tablespoon minced garlic
   (about 3 cloves)

1½ tablespoons minced
   peeled ginger
8 Roma tomatoes, chopped
2 cups cauliflower florets, cut
   into bite-size pieces
1½ cups red or brown lentils
6 cups water
4 cups baby spinach
Fresh cilantro, for garnish

1. In a small skillet, combine 1½ tablespoons of the oil and the mustard seeds, coriander seeds, turmeric, cumin seeds, and fennel seeds. Sauté over medium heat until the spices are fragrant and the seeds begin to pop, just under 5 minutes. Remove the pan from the heat and set aside.

2. In a large pot over medium heat, heat the remaining 1½ tablespoons oil and sauté the onion, garlic, and ginger until the onions just begin to brown, about 4 to 5 minutes. Add the tomatoes and cook, stirring occasionally, until the tomatoes release their juices and sugars, about 7 minutes. Add the cauliflower, lentils, and water. Bring to a boil, reduce the heat, cover, and cook until the lentils are tender, about 25 minutes. Stir in the spinach and the sautéed spices. Serve garnished with cilantro.

carrot ginger bisque

Carrots, the vibrant star of the show in this bisque, are valuable for their anti-oxidants, vitamins A and C, and fiber. The creaminess of this recipe is really due to the coconut milk. I like to beat the flu season by serving this soup often! As a parent, it is quite satisfying knowing that coconut milk is rich in minerals for bone building, such as magnesium, manganese, and phosphorus. Try serving this with the Quinoa Tabbouleh (page 66) or warm Quinoa Flatbread (page 8). I also like to serve it with the Red Bean and Rice Mini Cakes (page 59) or Black Bean Croquettes (page 55).

Makes 4 servings

2 tablespoons canola oil
1 medium onion, diced
1 clove garlic, minced
2 teaspoons grated peeled ginger
1 small Thai chile, chopped

9 large carrots, peeled and chopped
  (about 9 cups)
3 cups Vegetable Stock (page 19)
  or water
1 (12-ounce) can coconut milk
Sea salt

1. In a large pot over medium heat, heat the oil and sauté the onion, garlic, ginger, and chile until the onions start to brown, about 7 minutes. Add the carrots and stock. Bring to a gentle boil over high heat. Reduce the heat to medium-low and cook, covered, until the carrots are tender, about 20 minutes. Puree the soup until creamy, using an immersion blender, or in batches in a blender or food processor. Return the soup to the pot, stir in the milk, and season to taste with salt. Serve and enjoy!

creamy broccoli soup

This soup is a hit with children. It is creamy and mild while being packed with broccoli. Broccoli is a nutritional powerhouse for several reasons: it contains special anti-inflammatory properties that can decrease allergic responses, and copious amounts of vitamin K as well as vitamin A. We really enjoy this soup with the Sweet Potato and Beet Chips (page 76) and a thick slice of homemade bread.

Makes 6 servings

2 tablespoons canola oil

3 large leeks, white parts only, cleaned and cut into thin slices

2 cloves garlic, finely chopped

3 cups broccoli florets (about 2 medium heads)

1 cup cauliflower florets (about 1 small head)

½ cup peeled and diced new potato (about 1 small potato)

5 cups Walnut Almond Milk (page 18)

⅛ teaspoon ground nutmeg

Sea salt and freshly ground black pepper

1. In a large pot over medium heat, heat the oil and sauté the leeks for 5 minutes. Add the garlic and continue sautéing for another 5 minutes, stirring occasionally. Add the broccoli, cauliflower, potato, and milk. Bring to a gentle boil over high heat. Reduce the heat to medium-low and cook, covered, until the vegetables are tender, about 10 to 15 minutes. Puree the soup until creamy, using an immersion blender, or in batches in a blender or food processor. Add the nutmeg and season to taste with salt and pepper. Serve and enjoy!

cauliflower bisque

Here is another gorgeously creamy soup, gobbled up with delight by young and old alike! The pine nuts in particular add a rich, satisfying body to this bisque. I recommend serving this with either the Open-Face Cucumber Sandwich (page 51) or the Purple Potato Niçoise-Style Salad (page 111) and fresh-baked bread.

Makes 6 servings

2 teaspoons cumin seeds

2 tablespoons canola oil

1 large onion, diced

3 cloves garlic, finely chopped

2 large heads cauliflower, cut into florets

5½ cups Vegetable Stock (page 19)

½ cup pine nuts

Sea salt and freshly ground black pepper

½ cup chopped fresh cilantro (leaves only), for garnish

6 green onions, cut diagonally into thin slices, for garnish

1. In a small skillet over medium heat, toast the cumin seeds until they start to smell fragrant, about 5 minutes. Transfer to a plate to stop further toasting.

2. In a large pot over medium heat, heat the oil and sauté the onion for 5 minutes. Add the garlic and continue sautéing for another 5 minutes, stirring occasionally. Add the cauliflower and the stock. Bring to a gentle boil over high heat. Reduce the heat to medium-low and cook, covered, until the cauliflower is tender, about 15 to 20 minutes. Add the nuts and cumin seeds. Puree the soup until creamy, using an immersion blender, or in batches in a blender or food processor. Season to taste with salt and pepper. Serve in bowls garnished with fresh cilantro and green onions.

kale butternut squash bean soup

Butternut squash, packed with vitamin A, brings a subtle sweetness to this comforting, hearty, bone-building soup. Kale leaves have more vitamin K than any other vegetable. The cannellini beans add extra fiber, plus protein. For accompaniments, I recommend the bright and warm Beet Salad (page 109) or the Chinese Green Beans (page 98).

Makes 6 servings

3 tablespoons canola oil

1 large onion, diced

8 Roma tomatoes, chopped

½ teaspoon dried oregano

1 teaspoon dried marjoram

4 cloves garlic, finely chopped

1 large butternut squash, seeded, peeled, and cubed

8 cups Vegetable Stock (page 19)

6 cups stemmed, roughly chopped, and packed kale leaves

3 cups cooked cannellini beans, or 2 (15-ounce) cans, rinsed and drained

Sea salt and freshly ground black pepper

1. In a large pot over medium-low heat, heat the oil and sauté the onions until they have just started to brown, about 7 minutes. Add the tomatoes, oregano, and marjoram. Cook for 5 minutes, stirring occasionally. Add the garlic and sauté for just 1 minute before adding the squash and stock. Bring to a gentle boil over high heat. Reduce the heat to low and cook, covered, until the squash is tender and cooked through, about 30 minutes. Stir in the kale and beans and cook until the kale has softened and sweetened, about 10 minutes more. Season to taste with salt and pepper and serve.

black bean and poblano soup

Soft, warmed corn tortillas, wrapped up in a cloth to retain the heat, are the perfect accompaniment to this hearty, spicy soup, along with guacamole and the Pico de Gallo (page 21). For a side vegetable, the Raw Kale Salad (page 106) works really nicely, or simply shred cabbage and toss with olive oil, lime, cilantro, sea salt, and pine nuts. Black beans are one of nature's ideal foods. The ratio of protein to fiber in these beans, also high in phytonutrients, supports optimal digestion.

Makes 6 servings

1 poblano chile

1 green bell pepper

3 tablespoons pumpkin seeds

1 large dried ancho chile, stemmed
  and seeded

1 tablespoon canola oil

2 shallots, chopped

1 medium red onion, chopped

3 cloves garlic, minced

1 (14.5-ounce) can
  fire-roasted tomatoes

5½ cups Vegetable Stock (page 19)

2 cups peeled diced
  butternut squash

3 cups cooked black beans,
  or 2 (15-ounce) cans,
  rinsed and drained

Sea salt

Fresh cilantro, for garnish

1. Preheat the broiler. Broil the poblano chile and bell pepper on a foil-lined baking sheet. Rotate the baking sheet after 5 minutes and broil for another 5 minutes. The peppers will be charred when finished. Transfer to a bowl, cover immediately to trap the steam, and let rest for 15 minutes. Peel the peppers, remove the seeds, and chop into small pieces.

(continued)

2. In a medium skillet over medium heat, toast the pumpkin seeds until slightly browned, about 5 minutes. Immediately transfer to a plate to stop the toasting. In the same skillet over medium-high heat, toast the ancho chile until it becomes a few shades darker, about 1 minute. Remove from the heat.

3. In a medium saucepan, heat the oil and sauté the shallots, onion, and garlic, stirring occasionally, until they have softened and begun to brown, about 10 minutes.

4. Put the onion mixture, the tomatoes, and the ancho chile in a blender or food processor and process until smooth. Return this mixture to the saucepan over medium heat and cook, stirring, for about 8 minutes to thicken. Stir in the stock and squash and bring to a boil. Immediately reduce the heat to a simmer. Continue simmering, uncovered, for 20 minutes. Stir in the beans and the peppers. Cook, uncovered, for 5 minutes. Season to taste with salt. Ladle the soup into bowls, top with the toasted pumpkin seeds, and garnish with cilantro to serve.

Packed lunches became a lot more dynamic in our household once I started using thermoses! Nowadays there are plenty of high-quality stainless steel thermoses available. Hot soups and croquettes make for great meals that deliver lasting energy. It is important to heat food to 212 degrees F before packing in a thermos to prevent bacteria from growing. For a complete protein, pack a grain of some sort along with the bean soups. I recommend either a thick slice of the Sandwich Bread (page 7) or a round of Quinoa Flatbread (page 8). And always remember to pack a spoon!

powerful and simple
vegetable and bean soup

This soup is so pleasing aromatically, visually, and to the taste. The purple cabbage, yellow delicata squash, and vivid green parsley interact in just the right proportions to bring out each other's brightness. Red cabbage is one of the many powerful ingredients in this soup, and a supreme source for vitamins C and A. I love small red beans in this soup, but kidney beans are tasty too.

Makes 4 to 6 servings

1½ tablespoons extra-virgin olive oil

1 large yellow onion, finely chopped

1 large carrot, peeled and sliced into half-moons

1 celery stalk, finely chopped

1 delicata squash, washed, cut in half, seeded, and chopped into thin slices with the skin left on

2 cups very finely chopped red cabbage

2 cloves garlic, minced

6 cups Vegetable Stock (page 19)

1½ cups cooked red beans, or 1 (15-ounce) can, rinsed and drained

Kosher salt and freshly ground black pepper

3 tablespoons chopped fresh flat leaf parsley

1. In a large pot over medium heat, heat the oil and sauté the onion, carrot, and celery until softened, about 5 minutes. Add the squash, cabbage, and garlic. Cover the pot and cook for about 5 minutes. Add the stock and bring to a boil. Reduce the heat to a gentle simmer and add the beans. Continue simmering until all the vegetables are cooked through, about 45 minutes. Season to taste with salt and pepper. Ladle into bowls and garnish with a sprinkling of the parsley to serve.

italian wedding soup

Swirling the rich pesto into each bowl of brightly colored soup is such a pleasure. There is a profusion of white beans in this festive soup, a great source of macro minerals such as magnesium, calcium, phosphorus, and potassium, plus ample B vitamins. Choose your favorite white bean—borlotti, white lima, butter, and cannellini are good options. Accompany with the Heirloom Tomato Salad (page 108) and fresh-baked bread with high-quality extra-virgin olive oil for dipping.

Makes 4 to 6 servings

2 tablespoons extra-virgin olive oil

2 shallots, finely chopped

1 medium yellow onion, finely chopped

1 large carrot, peeled and chopped

1 small parsnip, chopped

1 celery stalk, chopped

5 Roma tomatoes, diced, with their juices

1 small yellow crookneck squash, sliced into half-moons

2 cloves garlic, finely chopped

6 cups Vegetable Stock (page 19)

3 cups cooked white beans, or 2 (15-ounce) cans, rinsed and drained

Sea salt and freshly ground black pepper

5 leaves curly kale, washed, stemmed, and cut into thin strips

2 tablespoons minced fresh flat leaf parsley

½ tablespoon chopped fresh oregano

½ cup pesto

1. In a large pot over medium heat, heat the oil and sauté the shallots, onion, carrot, parsnip, and celery until the vegetables are softened, about 5 minutes. Add the tomatoes, squash, and garlic. Cover the pot and cook, about 5 minutes. Add the stock and bring to a boil. Reduce the heat to a gentle simmer and add the beans. Continue simmering until all the vegetables are cooked through, about 15 minutes. Season to taste with salt and pepper. Add the kale and simmer, covered, until the kale softens, about 5 minutes more. To serve, garnish each bowl with a sprinkling of parsley and oregano and a dollop of pesto.

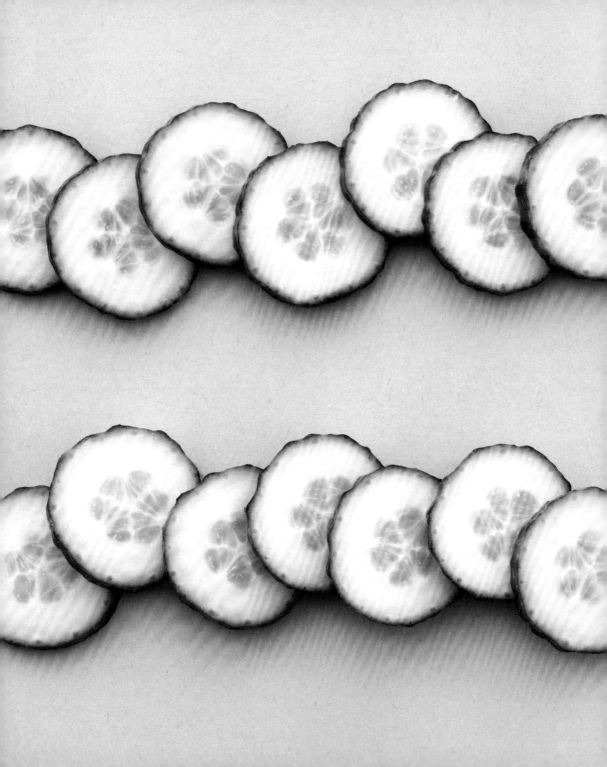

vegetables & salads

I RECOMMEND SERVING a large portion of vegetables—particularly dark leafy greens—with every lunch and dinner. If you can start your kids off this way, they expect vegetables without exception as part of their meals, and learn to appreciate the flavor and texture. I consider vegetables equally as important as the protein portion of the meal.

Vegetables offer a cornucopia of nutrients and fiber. They are essential to our immune system and help us live to our full potential by nourishing our overall strength and protecting us from cancer, heart disease, and diabetes. As an adult, my favorite lunch is a salad. Because these dishes weren't designed as the main meal, they don't provide complete protein, but one could add a serving of quinoa or beans and rice and call it good.

pakoras

A comforting blend of onions, yams, and sweet potatoes is suffused with warming spices and drenched in a batter of protein-rich chickpea flour before being fried to crisp perfection. These pakoras are a tasty way to feed your kids more onions, which help us bounce back from colds and coughs. Onions contain calcium, magnesium, sodium, potassium, and are a good source of vitamin C and dietary fiber.

Makes 4 to 6 servings as an appetizer

3 medium onions, peeled and diced

1 medium yam, peeled and diced

2 medium sweet potatoes, peeled and diced

1½ teaspoons sea salt

1 teaspoon chile powder

1 teaspoon garam masala

1 teaspoon turmeric

2 green chiles, finely chopped

1 teaspoon coriander seeds

2 teaspoons cumin seeds

2 cups chickpea flour

¾ cup cold water, plus more for thinning batter

2 tablespoons finely chopped fresh cilantro

Canola oil, for frying

Chutney, for serving

1. In a large bowl, combine the onions, yam, and sweet potatoes. Add the salt, chile powder, garam masala, turmeric, chiles, coriander, and cumin and mix with a wooden spoon. Add the chickpea flour and mix again.

2. Add the water to the mixture, then add a tablespoon more at a time as needed, stirring well, until a thick batter is formed. (The batter should be thick but drop easily from a spoon.) Add the cilantro and stir well.

3. Fill a large saucepan one-third full of oil. Heat the oil to 450 degrees F.

4. Test the heat by cooking just one pakora first. Use a soup spoon to put spoonfuls of the batter into the oil. Cook until golden brown, about 2 to 3 minutes. Remove with a slotted spoon and put on a clean kitchen towel or paper towel to drain. Serve hot with a favorite chutney.

chinese green beans

You can make this dish with any kind of green bean. However, I think it is worth the special trip to an Asian market for Chinese long beans. They are quite something—you can actually tie the ever-so-long beans into knots. These beans served with brown rice and steamed or fried tofu make a simple and very satisfying meal.

Makes 4 to 6 servings

1 tablespoon canola oil

4 shallots, thinly sliced

1 pound Chinese long or green beans, cut into 4-inch lengths

½ red bell pepper, seeded and cut into thin strips

1 small serrano chile, minced (optional)

1 teaspoon maple syrup

3 tablespoons water

2 tablespoons tamari

Freshly ground black pepper

1 tablespoon gomasio or toasted sesame seeds with sea salt

1. In a large sauté pan over medium heat, heat the oil and cook the shallots, covered, until browned and beginning to crisp, about 4 minutes. Add the beans, bell pepper, and chile and sauté until the beans and peppers start to blister slightly with brown spots, about 4 to 5 minutes. Drizzle in the maple syrup and water. Reduce the temperature to low and cook, covered, until the water has evaporated and the beans are tender, about 3 to 5 minutes. Add the tamari and pepper to taste, cooking for 2 to 3 minutes more. Transfer the beans to a serving platter, sprinkle with gomasio, and enjoy!

> Gomasio is a mixture of sesame seeds and dehydrated sea vegetables, popular in Japanese cooking.

bok choy with seeds

Bok choy has a distinctive flavor and texture, and is rich in vitamins A and K. It is very palatable for children, being milder than some of the other heartier greens. The toasty seeds topping this succulent dish make for an exciting crunch. The garlic adds flavor without being too intense.

Makes 4 servings

1 cup pumpkin seeds
½ cup sesame seeds
½ cup sunflower seeds
½ cup extra-virgin olive oil
Kosher salt
4 tablespoons canola oil
2 shallots, finely chopped

2½ tablespoons chopped garlic
4 tablespoons tamari
½ cup finely chopped shiitake
   mushrooms
1½ cups cherry tomatoes, halved
4 heads bok choy, cut into long thin
   strips from top to bottom

1. Preheat the oven to 350 degrees F. In a medium bowl, combine the pumpkin, sesame, and sunflower seeds with the olive oil. Spread the mixture evenly on a clean, dry baking sheet. Sprinkle with salt and toast in the oven for 8 to 10 minutes. Set on a rack to cool.

2. In a large sauté pan or wok, heat the canola oil. Sauté the shallots and garlic for 1 minute. Add the tamari and mushrooms and sauté until the mushrooms shrink and brown slightly. Add the tomatoes and cook until they release their juices, about 3 to 4 minutes. Add the bok choy and stir, being sure to coat each strip with the tamari mixture. Cook until the bok choy has just started to soften, about 2 to 3 minutes. Transfer the vegetable mixture to a serving bowl, top with the toasted seeds, and serve.

braised purple cabbage

If you don't have any red wine on hand or you don't consume alcohol, you can substitute apple juice or simply additional water. The red wine adds a unique complexity in depth of flavor, while apple juice adds a sweetness that appeals to younger taste buds. The liquid steams and braises the cabbage while deglazing the pan from the shallots and still allows the remaining ingredients to cook and retain their distinctive flavor in the finished dish. I find that shredding cabbage thinly is faster and easier with a serrated bread knife.

Makes 6 servings

2 tablespoons extra-virgin olive oil

4 medium shallots, chopped finely

2 pounds red cabbage (1 medium head), shredded

1 medium apple, chopped

½ cup red wine

⅓ cup water

Sea salt and freshly ground black pepper

1. In a large sauté pan or saucepan over medium heat, heat the oil and sauté the shallots until they just begin to brown, about 3 minutes. Add the cabbage, apple, wine, and water. Cook, covered, until the liquid has evaporated and the cabbage is soft and a rich, deep purple color, about 15 to 20 minutes. Season to taste with salt and pepper and serve.

broccolini with italian flair

Kids love the toasted bread crumbs coating the broccoli in this dish, and so do adults. Broccolini is called for in this recipe, however, broccoli is terrific too. Broccoli is really a choice vegetable to serve often, with its high levels of potassium, calcium, magnesium, beta carotene, and vitamins K and C.

Makes 4 servings

2 bunches broccolini

1 red bell pepper, seeded and thinly sliced

3½ tablespoons extra-virgin olive oil

Zest of ½ lemon

4 cloves garlic, minced

2 tablespoons freshly squeezed lemon juice

½ cup toasted gluten-free bread crumbs

2 tablespoons finely chopped fresh basil

¼ cup lightly toasted pine nuts

Sea salt and freshly ground black pepper

1. Trim 1½ inches of stem from the bottom of each broccolini floret. Bring a large pot of water to a boil and prepare an ice water bath. Add the broccolini and bell pepper to the pot and cook for 2 minutes. Drain the vegetables and immerse them in the water bath to halt the cooking.

2. In a large sauté pan over medium heat, heat the oil and sauté the lemon zest and garlic for a few moments. Drain the broccolini and bell pepper, pat dry, and put in the pan. Add the lemon juice, bread crumbs, basil, and pine nuts and toss to coat. Transfer to a serving dish, season to taste with salt and pepper, and serve.

brussels sprouts with shallots

This side dish offers an array of vibrant hues that will get your mouth watering. This is a nice choice to accompany the Shepherd's Pie (page 120). Brussels sprouts are *the* vegetable to eat more of. They offer generous amounts of sulfur, which enhances the immune system, as does their abundance of vitamin K.

Makes 6 servings

2 pounds brussels sprouts, trimmed and halved

1 medium carrot, peeled and cut into diagonal slices

4 tablespoons extra-virgin olive oil

1 red bell pepper, seeded and diced

1 cup finely chopped oyster mushrooms

½ cup thinly sliced shallots (about 4 medium shallots)

1 cup slivered almonds

Juice of ½ lemon

1 teaspoon sea salt, plus more for seasoning

2 tablespoons chopped fresh thyme

3 tablespoons chopped fresh chives

Freshly ground black pepper

1. In a large saucepan over high heat, steam the brussels sprouts and carrot over 2½ cups water until tender and easily pierced with a fork, about 10 to 15 minutes (most of the water should evaporate). Meanwhile, in a sauté pan over low heat, heat the oil and sauté the bell pepper, mushrooms, and shallots until they begin to brown, about 3 minutes.

2. In a small skillet over medium heat, toast the almonds until lightly browned. In a large serving bowl, combine the brussels sprouts mixture with the shallot mixture. Add the almonds, lemon juice, salt, thyme, and chives, mixing well. Season to taste with salt and pepper. Serve and enjoy while hot.

spinach salad

This salad offers sweet bursts of thinly sliced, juicy Asian pears and chewy dried cherries among tender greens, dressed with a citrus dressing and topped with toasted hazelnuts. The dressing, lightly sweetened with maple syrup, is a great way to attract youngsters to the fresh salad.

Makes 6 servings

2 cups lightly toasted hazelnuts, finely chopped, divided

1 cup dried cherries, divided

3 bunches spinach leaves, well washed and torn into bite-size pieces

2 Asian pears, cored and cut into very thin slices

2 shallots, cut into thin slices

⅛ cup freshly squeezed orange juice

1½ tablespoons white balsamic vinegar

⅓ cup extra-virgin olive oil

½ tablespoon maple syrup

½ teaspoon kosher salt

¼ teaspoon freshly ground black pepper

1. In a large mixing bowl, combine 1 cup of the hazelnuts, ½ cup of the cherries, and the spinach, pears, and shallots. In a small jar or bowl, thoroughly combine the orange juice, vinegar, oil, maple syrup, salt, and pepper. Toss with the spinach mixture. Divide the salad equally onto 6 salad plates. Before serving, distribute the remaining 1 cup hazelnuts and ½ cup cherries over each plate, for a delicious garnish.

Spinach is rewarding to grow and requires minimal effort. If you have a little gardening space, why not grow spinach in trays on your deck railing or
in window boxes? Because spinach is shallow-rooted, it is not necessary to
plant it in a deep pot. Spinach just requires nutrient-rich, fast-draining soil.
Before planting your spinach, soak the seeds in filtered water for 24 hours.
Next, sow the seeds ½-inch deep and 3 inches apart. Once the baby spinach
plants emerge and put out their first true leaves, thin out to a spacing of 6 to
8 inches. Be sure to water whenever the soil dries out to the depth of your first
knuckle and, about once a month, add some dried-out compost or water with
compost tea. Fresh-picked spinach is a joy, and with a cut-and-come-again
approach, you can have many fresh harvests. Be sure to use scissors when
clipping leaves the first time around, so as not to disturb the shallow roots.

raw kale salad

Although raw, the greens are tender, as they are thinly sliced and gently massaged to slightly break them down. The dressing is just a smidgen sweet with maple syrup added to tamari, lemon juice, and sesame oil. The avocado is also massaged into the julienned kale, making a creamy backdrop to the crisp leaves. Raw kale can provide even more nutrients than cooked kale, especially zinc. Foods with zinc are great to have in your kitchen "medicine cabinet," as they really fuel the immune system. That's especially empowering for parents, whose active kids are often exposed to cold bugs.

Makes 6 servings

1 bunch kale

1½ tablespoons freshly squeezed
   lemon juice

2 tablespoons tamari

1 tablespoon maple syrup

1 tablespoon sesame oil

2 scallions, finely chopped

2 cloves garlic, minced

1 teaspoon sea salt

1 tablespoon grated peeled ginger

1 avocado, diced, divided

1 orange bell pepper, seeded
   and diced

3 shallots, minced

¾ cup cherry tomatoes, halved

2 tablespoons gomasio (optional),
   (see note, page 98)

1. Thoroughly wash the kale leaves and pat dry. Remove the central ribs and finely chop the leaves, setting them aside in a large bowl. To make the dressing, in a small bowl, combine the lemon juice, tamari, maple syrup, oil, scallions, garlic, salt, and ginger. Add the dressing to the kale and massage well with clean hands until wilted, about 5 minutes. Add half of the avocado and continue to massage for 1 minute more. Add the remaining half of avocado, bell pepper, shallots, and tomatoes. Lightly toss to combine. Sprinkle the salad with gomasio and serve.

Kale is very easy to grow—in fact, you can start growing kale anytime between the very beginning of spring and the beginning of fall. After the seedlings have produced their first true leaves, thin to 8 inches apart. Kale loves to be watered regularly and appreciates a blanket of mulch. There are so many varieties of kale; it is a joy to get acquainted with all of their greenish, blue, and purple shades, their curly or pointy shapes, and their different tastes. If you live in the city, you can grow a satisfying crop of kale in a container. You will need a pot that provides at least a 6-inch diameter space per plant and a balance of sunlight and partial shade.

heirloom tomato salad

I've recently seen some daring takes on this salad, like the inclusion of sliced nectarines. The result is really dynamic, tangy, and sweet. If you feel like giving it a go, replace one pound of the tomatoes with one pound of sliced nectarines. You can create a beautiful pattern on the serving platter while feasting on the bright colors of summer.

Makes 6 servings

2 pounds assorted heirloom
    tomatoes
3 tablespoons extra-virgin olive oil
1 tablespoon balsamic vinegar
Sea salt and freshly ground
    black pepper

2 tablespoons minced chives
2 tablespoons finely chopped
    fresh basil
1 tablespoon chopped fresh oregano

1. Begin by cutting the larger tomatoes into ¼-inch-thick slices and the smaller tomatoes into halves. Arrange the tomatoes on a serving platter, such as a wide-rimmed shallow bowl or large plate. Drizzle the oil over the tomatoes, followed by the vinegar. Season to taste with salt and pepper. Top with a final sprinkling of the fresh herbs, equally distributed. Serve at room temperature.

beet salad

Enjoy red or golden beets in this salad, or a combination of the two. Red beets tend to be sweeter and more earthy; golden beets are milder. As a lover of greens, I occasionally double the amount of beet greens in the recipe. If you do this, season with a little more salt and olive oil. The beet root is a rich source of B-complex vitamins and minerals like iron, manganese, copper, and magnesium. The greens carry an impressive amount of lutein, which is good for eye health, and vitamin C.

Makes 4 servings

4 medium unpeeled beets, plus
   greens
3 cloves garlic, peeled
½ teaspoon sea salt
½ cup extra-virgin olive oil
3 tablespoons balsamic vinegar
1 tablespoon minced fresh oregano
Freshly ground black pepper

1½ cups cooked navy beans,
   or 1 (15-ounce) can,
   rinsed and drained
4 shallots, finely chopped
1 bunch Swiss chard, stems and
   center ribs removed
½ cup lightly toasted pine nuts

1. Trim the greens from the beets and wash everything; set aside the greens. Bring a large pot of water to a boil over high heat, add the beets, reduce the heat, and simmer until tender, about 30 minutes. Cut the beets into ½-inch-thick wedges and set aside.

2. Mash the garlic and salt together with a mortar and pestle. Put the garlic in a large bowl. Add the oil, vinegar, oregano, and pepper and whisk to incorporate. Add the beets, beans, and shallots. Toss lightly. Marinate at room temperature while preparing the greens.

3. Steam the greens and chard until tender, but still bright green, about 5 minutes. With a slotted spoon, transfer the greens mixture to a cutting board and chop into 1-inch pieces. Add the mixture to the beets and toss again. Transfer the salad to a serving platter, sprinkle with the pine nuts, and serve.

purple potato niçoise-style salad

This recipe calls for purple potatoes mainly because their color is so unusual and attractive. Unfortunately, not all markets carry these gems, as they are somewhat seasonal. You can substitute new potatoes for the purple potatoes with equally tasty results.

Makes 4 to 6 servings

2 cups quartered purple potatoes

3 tablespoons extra-virgin olive oil, divided

1½ tablespoons chopped fresh rosemary

Sea salt and freshly ground black pepper

2 cups green beans, ends trimmed

6 to 8 cups mixed greens

1 cup cherry tomatoes, halved

2 shallots, finely chopped

1 tablespoon fresh tarragon leaves

2 tablespoons finely chopped chives

Juice of 1 medium lemon

1½ teaspoons whole grain mustard

1 teaspoon maple syrup

½ cup crumbled Almond Feta Cheese (page 16)

1. Preheat the oven to 400 degrees F. Line a baking sheet with parchment paper. In a large bowl, toss the potatoes with 1 tablespoon of the oil, and the rosemary, salt, and pepper. Transfer the potato mixture to the baking sheet. Roast until lightly browned, about 40 minutes. Transfer to a large plate to cool while preparing the rest of the salad.

2. Bring a large pot of water to a boil. Put the beans in the pot and cook for 1½ minutes. Drain in a colander and run under cold water to stop the cooking. Pat dry.

3. In a large salad bowl, combine the greens, tomatoes, beans, shallots, tarragon, and chives. In a small bowl, whisk together the remaining 2 tablespoons oil, lemon juice, mustard, and maple syrup. Season to taste with salt and pepper. Pour the dressing over the vegetables and toss to combine. Divide among 4 to 6 serving bowls or plates, surround each with potatoes, top with cheese, and serve.

sweet potato oven fries

When you're making the Red Bean Burgers (page 45), these big, hearty fries are the ideal sidekick. Sweet potatoes have a lot going for them—they are high in vitamin B6, which our bodies need to absorb vitamin B12—both key ingredients for making red blood cells and immune cells. Feel free to add spices if desired; for example, we like to add one tablespoon chile powder and a pinch of cayenne when tossing with oil and salt before baking.

Makes 4 to 6 servings

2 large sweet potatoes, scrubbed
and cut into ¾-inch-thick slices
4 tablespoons extra-virgin olive oil

Sea salt and freshly ground
black pepper

1. Preheat the oven to 450 degrees F. In a large bowl, toss the potatoes with the oil. Add salt and pepper to taste. Transfer to a large baking sheet in a single layer, leaving space around each fry. Bake for 15 minutes, flip the fries with tongs or a spatula, and bake for an additional 10 minutes. Serve hot.

dinners

HAVING DINNER TOGETHER AS A FAMILY is a great time to connect over nourishing food. I find it is extra special when dinner preparation is shared by family members. If guests are joining your family, this prep can be fun but busy. Between tidying the home and cooking a feast, there is a lot to do! So when it comes to helping, the more the merrier. Kids can be very helpful with chopping vegetables, and they really enjoy the tactile experience. Younger ones are safe with a butter knife and soft vegetables such as mushrooms; older kids can do more demanding prep work and the occasional stirring that is part of many recipes.

Engaging the youngest kids with noncooking chores allows the cooks to focus. One fun way for the younger ones to be involved and feel a real sense of participation is to have them make place mats and place cards with construction paper, glue, paints, and markers. Let them surprise you and the guests!

On family-only nights, when everyone is hungry and the younger ones are on the verge of a meltdown, consider making some of the less labor-intensive meals, such as the Lentil Tacos (page 117), Black Bean Burgers (page 154), or Tamale Pie (page 152). If you decide to use store-bought pizza sauce, the Pizza (page 137) is another one that comes together fairly quickly.

The dinners here are designed to provide complete protein, with just a few exceptions. In those recipe notes you will see my recommendations for what to serve along with the dish. It might be something as simple as steamed quinoa, millet, forbidden rice, or the Quinoa Flatbread (page 8).

lentil tacos

I took inspiration for this delectable taco recipe from the renowned Isa Chandra. Beluga lentils, the main filling ingredient, are a bit different from other lentils: they are smaller and a deep purplish black, and they keep their shape when they cook, more so than other lentils. Their deep pigment indicates powerful antioxidants. Serving them with taco shells or corn tortillas makes a complete protein. Note that you can adjust the hot sauce to an appropriate spiciness for youngsters.

Makes 4 to 6 servings

1½ cups dried beluga lentils
   (French lentils or gray-green
   lentils work too)
4½ cups water
3 tablespoons canola oil, plus more
   for oiling
1 medium red onion, finely chopped
2 cups chopped stemmed shiitake
   mushrooms
3 cloves garlic, minced
1 tablespoon tamari
½ teaspoon dried oregano
1 tablespoon chile powder

1½ teaspoons ground cumin
½ teaspoon ground coriander
¾ teaspoon kosher salt
4 tablespoons tomato paste
2 tablespoons hot sauce
Pico de Gallo (page 21), for serving
Fresh cilantro, for serving
Lime slices, for serving
1 avocado, sliced, for serving
Chopped romaine, for serving
12 corn tortillas or taco shells,
   for serving

1. Rinse the lentils and put them in a large pot with the water. Bring to a boil over medium-high heat. Reduce the heat to medium-low and cover. Cook until the lentils are tender and have absorbed most of the water, about 20 minutes. Set aside.

(continued)

2. In a large sauté pan over medium heat, heat the oil and sauté the onion, mushrooms, garlic, and tamari until the onions just begin to brown, about 5 to 6 minutes. Stir in the oregano, chile powder, cumin, coriander, and salt and sauté for about 1 minute more. Add the lentils, tomato paste, and hot sauce to the pan and stir to combine. Cook for about 5 minutes more, stirring occasionally. Reduce the heat to low and cover to keep the taco filling warm. You may need to add a tablespoon or so of water (to keep it from thickening or drying out too much) from time to time while getting the rest of the meal on the table.

3. Arrange bowls of pico de gallo, cilantro, lime, avocado, and lettuce on the table for everyone to assemble their tacos with. If using fresh corn tortillas rather than taco shells, warm a large skillet over medium heat and lightly oil. Warm each tortilla for 30 seconds on each side and keep wrapped up in a napkin until all the tortillas are ready. Enjoy!

shepherd's pie

This makes a fantastic Thanksgiving entrée. As a comfort food I recommend the yam, sweet potato, and parsnip topping as a side dish on its own. This entrée goes beautifully with the Brussels Sprouts with Shallots (page 103) side dish. To make it a complete protein, consider replacing three-quarters cup of the lentils with an equal amount of quinoa.

Makes 6 servings

1¼ pounds sweet potatoes
  (about 2 large)
1¼ pounds yams (about 2 large)
5 parsnips, peeled and chopped
  into ½-inch pieces
1 tablespoon canola oil
1¼ teaspoons dried
  rosemary, divided
Sea salt
3 cups water
1½ cups dry French green lentils
¾ cup Walnut Almond Milk (page 18)
3 tablespoons extra-virgin
  olive oil, divided

Freshly ground black pepper
1 large yellow onion, sliced into
  thin half-moons
4 cloves garlic, minced
2 large carrots, peeled and sliced
  into thin half-moons
6 ounces shiitake mushrooms, sliced
8 leaves or 1 bunch curly green
  kale, stemmed and torn into
  bite-size pieces
½ teaspoon dried thyme
½ cup Vegetable Stock (page 19)

1. Preheat the oven to 400 degrees F. Wrap the sweet potatoes and yams in foil and bake for 30 minutes. Meanwhile, toss the parsnips with the canola oil, ½ teaspoon of the rosemary, and salt. Put the parsnips on a baking sheet and roast in the oven alongside the potatoes and yams for another 30 minutes. Stir the parsnips with a spatula about halfway through the roasting.

2. While the root vegetables are baking, bring the water to a boil. Add the lentils, reduce the heat to a simmer, and cover. Cook until the lentils are soft and most of the water has been absorbed, 20 to 25 minutes. Drain, discarding any extra liquid.

3. Remove the root vegetables from the oven and reduce the temperature to 350 degrees F. Scoop out the sweet potato and yam flesh into a medium bowl and discard the skins. Add the parsnips, milk, and 1 tablespoon of the olive oil. Mash with a potato masher to a smooth consistency. Season to taste with salt and pepper.

4. In a large pan over medium heat, heat the remaining 2 tablespoons olive oil and sauté the onion and garlic until the onions soften and just begin to brown, about 7 minutes. Add the carrots, mushrooms, and kale. Cook, stirring occasionally with a wooden spoon, until the vegetables soften, about 7 minutes more. Add the lentils along with the remaining ¾ teaspoon rosemary, the thyme, and stock. Cook for 5 minutes more to warm everything through. Season to taste with salt and pepper. Transfer the lentil and vegetable filling to a casserole dish. Spread the potato mixture over the lentil filling. Bake for 20 minutes and serve piping hot.

red bean rapini savory pie

This pie has got it all! It supplies complete protein, the red beans and rapini (also known as broccoli rabe) provide quality iron, and the overall fiber content is high. Like kale, rapini is a superb bone-strengthening food. If you sense rapini will be too bitter-tasting for the younger ones, substitute baby broccoli. I recommend serving this savory pie with the Heirloom Tomato Salad (page 108) and Italian Wedding Soup (page 92).

Makes 4 to 6 servings

1 cup brown rice flour
⅔ cup medium-grind cornmeal
½ teaspoon kosher salt, plus more
   for seasoning
½ cup canola oil
¾ cup chopped toasted
   walnuts, divided
1 medium bunch rapini, tough
   stems removed

2½ tablespoons extra-virgin olive oil
3 garlic cloves, minced
2 Roma tomatoes, chopped
2 cups cooked red beans, or 2 cups
   from 2 (15-ounce) cans, rinsed
   and drained
1 teaspoon minced fresh rosemary
Freshly ground black pepper

1. To make the crust, preheat the oven to 375 degrees F. In a food processor, combine the flour, cornmeal, salt, and canola oil until the dough holds together. Add ½ cup of the walnuts and pulse just until they are incorporated. Press the crust into a 9-inch tart pan or pie plate and bake until the crust is golden-brown and firm to the touch, about 35 minutes.

2. To make the filling, bring a large pot of salted water to a rolling boil. Add the rapini and cook until tender, about 5 minutes. Drain the rapini, run under cold water, and drain again. Coarsely chop and set aside.

3. In a large skillet over medium heat, heat the olive oil and sauté the garlic briefly, just under 1 minute. Stir in the tomatoes, cooking until they have softened, about 3 to 4 minutes. Add the beans, rosemary, and the rapini. Season to taste with salt and pepper. Continue to cook the filling until heated through. Fill the prepared tart crust with the hot filling, sprinkle with the remaining ¼ cup walnuts, cut into wedges, and serve immediately.

spring risotto torte

This torte is a little different from other risotto tortes, as the quinoa combined with arborio rice increases the protein content of the dish. I really love how this dish holds such a beautiful shape—the wedges of torte present so attractively! The porcini mushrooms add an earthy savor and also energize the immune system. Good accompaniments are the warm Beet Salad (page 109) or Broccolini with Italian Flair (page 102). Note that you can complete most of the steps the day before and reheat the torte just before serving.

Makes 6 to 8 servings

¼ cup plus 1 tablespoon extra-virgin olive oil, divided

½ cup gluten-free bread crumbs

4 cups water

2 ounces dried porcini mushrooms

1 pound asparagus

2 medium onions

3 cloves garlic, minced

1 cup arborio rice, rinsed to remove extra starch

¾ cup quinoa, rinsed

1½ cups white wine

Kosher salt and freshly ground black pepper

½ cup finely chopped fresh flat leaf parsley, for garnish

1. Lightly oil an 8-inch springform pan with 1 tablespoon of the oil and coat with the bread crumbs, shaking out the excess.

2. In a 1-quart saucepan, bring the water to a boil. Remove from the heat and soak the mushrooms for 1 hour. Gently lift the mushrooms out of the water, being careful not to stir up any grit that may have settled at the bottom of the pan. Squeeze the mushrooms dry, coarsely chop, and set aside. Line a fine mesh sieve with cheesecloth or a paper towel and drain the mushroom soaking liquid through it. In a small saucepan, bring the liquid to a simmer, maintaining the simmer until adding later.

3. Trim off and discard the tough ends of the asparagus. Chop the asparagus into 1-inch pieces. Lightly steam in a steaming basket over high heat for 5 minutes.

4. In a large soup pot over medium-low heat, heat the remaining ¼ cup oil and sauté the onions and garlic for 10 minutes. Add the mushrooms and cook for another 2 minutes. Then add the rice and quinoa and cook, stirring, until the grains become lightly translucent, about 7 minutes. Increase the heat to medium-high and add the wine and salt. Cook, stirring continuously, until the wine is almost completely absorbed, about 15 minutes. Add a ladleful of stock and continue to cook, stirring continuously, until it is all absorbed. Continue this process until all the stock is absorbed into the rice, about 30 to 40 minutes. Test a bit of rice; it should be tender yet firm. Remove the risotto from the heat and stir in the asparagus. Season to taste with pepper and additional salt.

5. Spoon the risotto into the prepared pan and smooth with a spatula. Let the risotto cool completely before placing it in the refrigerator overnight, or proceed to bake.

6. When ready to bake the torte, preheat the oven to 375 degrees F. Bake until heated all the way through, about 30 minutes. Carefully unmold the torte onto a serving platter and cut into wedges. Garnish the wedges with parsley and serve.

cassoulet

This traditional Provençal bean dish cooked in earthenware is so aromatic and utterly mouthwatering. It is full of protein from the white beans and bread crumbs. The root vegetables, leafy greens, and tomatoes offer lots of vitamin C. The Purple Potato Niçoise-Style Salad (page 111) is a lovely accompaniment to this dish.

Makes 6 servings

3 tablespoons extra-virgin olive oil, plus more for oiling

1 large red onion, diced

2 cups finely chopped shiitake mushrooms

1 large carrot, peeled and cut into ¼-inch-thick half-moons

1 large parsnip, cut into ¼-inch-thick half-moons

4 cloves garlic, finely chopped

2 teaspoons Dijon mustard

1½ tablespoons miso paste dissolved in 2 tablespoons hot water

½ teaspoon dried marjoram

¾ teaspoon dried thyme

1 large bay leaf

Sea salt and freshly ground black pepper

3 cups cooked white or speckled beans (like cannellini, navy, or berlotti), or 2 (15-ounce) cans, rinsed and drained

2 cups Vegetable Stock (page 19)

1¼ cups diced fresh tomatoes

2 cups baby spinach

2 cups torn Swiss chard leaves

¾ cup toasted gluten-free bread crumbs

¼ cup chopped fresh flat leaf parsley, leaves only, for garnish

Sprigs of fresh thyme, for garnish

1. Heat the oven to 350 degrees F. In a large skillet over medium heat, heat the oil and sauté the onion, mushrooms, carrot, and parsnip for about 5 minutes. Add the garlic and sauté briefly.

(continued)

2. In a small bowl, combine the mustard and miso. Add the miso mixture to the vegetables along with the marjoram, thyme, and bay leaf. Season to taste with salt and pepper.

3. Lightly oil a casserole dish or Dutch oven. Add the vegetable mixture, beans, stock, tomatoes, spinach, and chard and stir to combine well.

4. Cover and bake for 40 minutes. Remove the bay leaf, sprinkle with bread crumbs, and return to the oven to bake, uncovered, for 7 minutes. Garnish with parsley and thyme sprigs and serve.

polenta quinoa amaranth stacks with roasted vegetables

This polenta-quinoa-amaranth grain combination with red beans is not only tasty, but also provides complete protein. Amaranth has a strong flavor, so a little is all you need. I encourage you to add amaranth to other grain dishes, as it is very high in protein—including lysine, which helps us absorb calcium and metabolize fatty acids—and has twice as much calcium as dairy milk.

Makes 4 to 6 servings

1½ cups medium-grind
   yellow cornmeal
2 tablespoons amaranth
¼ cup quinoa
7 cups water
2 teaspoons sea salt, plus more
   for seasoning
1 tablespoon extra-virgin olive oil,
   plus more for oiling and brushing
1 cup cooked small red or kidney
   beans, or 1 cup from 1 (15-ounce)
   can, rinsed and drained

Freshly ground black pepper
4 medium beets, peeled and cut
   into thin slices
1 delicata squash, halved, seeded,
   and cut into thin slices
1 large parsnip, cut into matchsticks
1 small fennel bulb, trimmed and
   cut into bite-size slices
8 cloves garlic, peeled and halved
3 tablespoons canola oil

1. In a small bowl, combine the cornmeal, amaranth, and quinoa. In a large saucepot, bring the water to a boil. Reduce the heat to medium and add the salt. Pour the grains into the water in a slow stream, stirring constantly. Reduce the temperature to low and cook, stirring frequently, until a stiff consistency is reached, about 30 to 40 minutes. Stir in the olive oil and the beans. Season to taste with additional salt and pepper.

(continued)

2. Lightly oil a 12-inch square baking pan with olive oil. Pour in the polenta and bean mixture and smooth out the surface with a spatula, spreading evenly. Put in the refrigerator to set, about 1 hour.

3. Meanwhile, preheat the oven to 450 degrees F. Put the beets, squash, parsnip, fennel, and garlic in a large bowl and toss with the canola oil. Season to taste with salt and pepper. Spread the vegetables evenly on a baking sheet. Roast the vegetables for 20 minutes, turning with a spatula about halfway through. Increase the oven temperature to 500 degrees F and roast the vegetables for 10 minutes more. Remove from the oven and keep warm by covering with foil.

4. To bake the polenta, reduce the oven temperature to 375 degrees F. Lightly oil a baking sheet with olive oil. Cut the polenta into 4 squares, or 6 rectangles, and put them on the baking sheet. Brush the tops with additional olive oil and bake until golden and piping hot, about 15 to 20 minutes. Serve topped with the roasted vegetables.

spaghetti squash alla puttanesca

This is a deliciously different puttanesca sauce. I hope Italians approve of the liberties I've taken to expand on the traditional ingredients, in an effort to boost the protein (by including white beans) and the proportion of vitamin A–rich greens (with ample spinach), plus meaty shiitake mushrooms for immune system support. For complete protein, serve with Quinoa Flatbread (page 8). I recommend the Broccolini with Italian Flair (page 102) as a side dish.

Makes 4 to 6 servings

2 medium spaghetti squashes

2 tablespoons canola oil, plus more for oiling

1 large yellow onion, diced

2 cups shiitake mushrooms, thinly sliced

5 cloves garlic, minced

2 (14.5-ounce) cans crushed tomatoes

½ cup tomato paste

1 cup kalamata olives, pitted and cut in half

3 tablespoons capers

1 teaspoon crushed red pepper flakes

1½ teaspoons dried oregano

1 teaspoon dried basil

2 cups cooked white beans (like berlotti, cannellini, or navy), or 2 cups from 2 (15-ounce) cans, rinsed and drained

4 cups loosely packed baby spinach leaves

Kosher salt and freshly ground black pepper

2 tablespoons extra-virgin olive oil

¼ cup chopped fresh flat leaf parsley, for garnish

1. Preheat the oven to 350 degrees F. Lightly oil 2 baking sheets. Cut the spaghetti squashes in half lengthwise. Scrape out the seeds with a spoon and discard the seeds. Put the squashes cut side down on the baking sheets.

(continued)

Bake until a knife can be inserted with ease, about 35 minutes. Remove from the oven and set aside.

2. Meanwhile, prepare the sauce. In a large sauté pan over medium heat, heat the canola oil and sauté the onion and mushrooms. Add the garlic and sauté for 2 minutes. Stir in the tomatoes, tomato paste, olives, capers, red pepper flakes, oregano, and basil. Cook for 10 minutes. Stir in the beans and spinach. Cook until the spinach wilts, about 3 to 4 minutes. Thin the sauce by adding ⅔ cup of water. Season to taste with salt and pepper.

3. Use a large metal spoon or fork to scoop the spaghetti-like pulp from the squash halves. Toss with the olive oil and season to taste with salt and pepper. Divide the "spaghetti" among 4 shallow bowls and ladle the puttanesca sauce on top. Garnish with a sprinkling of parsley.

zucchini piccata

Dipping batter-drenched baked zucchini strips into marinara is not only tasty—it is fun! My favorite health booster of this dish is the zucchini batter. It is loaded with sesame seeds, sunflower seeds, pumpkin seeds, hemp seeds, and pine nuts. These seeds offer lots of vitamin E, protein, minerals, and zinc. The pine nuts are a great source of iron—especially if you offer a bowlful on the table. The sesame seeds in the tahini are a lovely source of calcium. You can serve this with store-bought marinara in a pinch. If you opt for homemade marinara, be sure to make it first, before the piccata.

Makes 6 servings

5 tablespoons water

6 tablespoons extra-virgin olive oil, divided

2 tablespoons tahini

2 tablespoons cashew butter

2 teaspoons freshly squeezed lemon juice

1½ tablespoons finely chopped fresh basil

1½ tablespoons finely chopped fresh parsley

½ cup gluten-free and vegan cracker crumbs (such as Mary's Gone Crackers)

¼ cup raw sunflower seeds

⅛ cup raw pine nuts

⅛ cup raw pumpkin seeds

½ tablespoon hemp seeds

½ tablespoon sesame seeds

½ teaspoon baking powder

1 teaspoon sea salt

½ teaspoon freshly ground black pepper

4 large zucchini, each halved and the halves cut into 4 to 6 strips

Marinara Sauce (page 20), for dipping

1. Preheat the oven to 400 degrees F and line a large baking sheet with parchment paper.

(continued)

2. In a medium mixing bowl, combine the water, 2 tablespoons of the oil, and the tahini, cashew butter, lemon juice, basil, and parsley.

3. In a food processor, combine the cracker crumbs, sunflower seeds, pine nuts, pumpkin seeds, hemp seeds, sesame seeds, baking powder, salt, and pepper. Pulse until the seeds are ground into a coarse flour. Transfer to a bowl.

4. Line up the tahini batter bowl, the crumb mixture bowl, and the baking sheet. Place each zucchini strip in the batter and then dip it into the crumb mixture until well coated, then put it on the pan.

5. After all the strips have been dipped and coated, drizzle the remaining 4 tablespoons oil over the strips and bake until the coating is slightly browned, about 20 minutes. Serve with the marinara sauce for dipping.

pizza

Building pizzas can be such a pleasure for the family. Younger kids can take pride in rolling out the dough and sprinkling on the toppings. Tomatoes deliver more of the antioxidant lycopene than any other fruit or vegetable, plus vitamins A, C, and K. The pizza is topped with superfood kale, immune-boosting porcini mushrooms, and almond cheese abundant in protein and bone-nourishing phosphorus.

Makes two 10-inch pizzas

3 tablespoons extra-virgin olive oil, divided, plus more for brushing
1 small red onion, chopped
6 cloves garlic, coarsely chopped
6 pounds vine-ripened tomatoes, cut into eighths
2 cups packed fresh basil leaves
⅓ cup chopped fresh oregano
1 medium carrot, peeled and grated
1¼ teaspoons sea salt, plus more for seasoning
Freshly ground black pepper
3¾ cups cold water, divided
1 cup medium-grind cornmeal, plus more for dusting

⅛ cup amaranth
⅛ cup quinoa
1 red onion, cut into thin half-moons
2 cloves garlic, minced
½ cup dried porcini mushrooms, reconstituted by soaking in boiled water for 30 minutes, drained, and thinly sliced
1 bunch lacinato kale, cut into fine ribbons
1 cup Almond Feta Cheese (page 16)
1 cup cherry tomatoes, halved
½ cup pine nuts

1. To make the sauce, in a large saucepan over medium heat, heat 1 tablespoon of the oil and sauté the onion and garlic for 2 minutes, being careful not to brown the garlic. Add the tomatoes, basil, oregano, and carrot. Stir occasionally as the tomatoes release their liquid. When the mixture reaches a low boil, reduce the heat and simmer until most, but not all, of the liquid has evaporated,

(continued)

up to 10 minutes. Puree the sauce until it has a smooth consistency, using an immersion blender, or in batches in a blender or food processor.

2. Return the sauce to the pan. Over medium heat, return the sauce to a boil, reduce the temperature to low, and simmer until the sauce thickens. Season to taste with salt and pepper. Let the sauce cool as you make the pizza dough.

3. To make the dough, in a medium saucepan over medium-high heat, bring 2¾ cups of the water to a boil. In a medium bowl, combine the cornmeal, amaranth, quinoa, and salt. Add the remaining 1 cup water to the grains mixture and whisk to combine. Very slowly add the mixture to the boiling water, whisking constantly. Return the mixture to a boil, still whisking, then immediately reduce the heat to medium-low and cook, stirring, until thickened and soft, about 15 minutes.

4. Line 2 baking sheets with parchment paper and dust with cornmeal. Pour half of the dough into the center of each pan. With wet hands, work the dough into 2 circles about 10 inches in diameter. Refrigerate for 30 minutes or until firm.

5. Preheat the oven to 375 degrees F. Brush the dough with olive oil and bake for 35 minutes. Set aside the baked crust while preparing the pizza toppings.

6. To assemble the pizzas, keep the oven at 375 degrees F. In a large skillet, heat the remaining 2 tablespoons oil and sauté the onion and garlic until the onion is softened, about 5 minutes. Add the mushrooms and sauté for 4 minutes longer. Add the kale and continue sautéing until the kale wilts slightly, about 3 minutes. Remove from the heat and set aside.

7. Spread the pizza sauce over the crusts and divide the vegetables evenly between the two pizzas. Evenly distribute the feta over each pizza. Then, scatter the tomatoes and pine nuts over each pizza. Season to taste with salt and pepper. Bake for 15 minutes and serve slices while hot!

Pesto pizzas are another mouthwatering way to go! To make a pesto pizza, follow the same instructions for the crust but substitute pesto for the red tomato sauce. You also might enjoy using the Quinoa Flatbread (page 8) as the crust to make 8 individual pizzas (4 to 6 inches in diameter). Once the dough is flattened and shaped, top with either pesto or tomato sauce, follow with the toppings, and bake at 375 degrees F for about 17 minutes.

kebabs

Kebabs are such a festive summer food. The whole family will enjoy having a meal cooked on the grill. You might want to grill up some extra vegetables that have been marinating too! We always throw onion rings on the grill; they sweeten up tremendously as their sugars come to the surface over the hot coals. These kebabs are flush with protein-packed tempeh and abounding in vitamin-rich vegetables. When it comes to choosing a rice to serve the kebabs on, black forbidden rice is my favorite; I think it's the tastiest, and it is arguably the most nutritious.

Makes 4 servings

2 tablespoons extra-virgin olive oil

1 small red onion, minced

2 cloves garlic

4 cups chopped fresh tomatoes

⅓ cup maple syrup

¼ cup blackstrap molasses

½ cup apple cider vinegar

2 teaspoons mustard powder

1 teaspoon chile powder

1 teaspoon sea salt

1 teaspoon freshly ground black pepper

⅛ to ¼ teaspoon paprika

4 wooden skewers

8 crimini or button mushrooms

12 shiitake mushrooms

12 cherry tomatoes

1 small orange bell pepper, seeded and cut into bite-size pieces

2 small baby bok choy, leaves separated

1 yellow summer squash, cut into bite-size pieces

1 (8-ounce) package tempeh, cut into bite-size pieces

Cooked rice, for serving

1. To make the sauce, in a large saucepan or Dutch oven, heat the oil and sauté the onion and garlic until softened and transparent, about 5 minutes. Add the tomatoes, maple syrup, molasses, vinegar, mustard powder, chile powder, salt, pepper, and paprika to the saucepan. Bring to a boil and reduce the

(continued)

heat to low. Cook, uncovered, for 1 hour. Puree the sauce, using an immersion blender, or in batches in a blender or food processor. Return the sauce to the saucepan and continue simmering for 30 minutes more. Remove from the heat and let cool.

2. Prepare the wooden skewers by soaking them in water for 15 minutes. Preheat the grill to medium heat. Skewer the vegetables and tempeh in a colorful pattern. Brush the kebabs generously with the sauce. Grill the kebabs for 3 minutes on each side. You may need to brush the kebabs with more sauce after flipping to the other side. The kebabs are ready when the vegetables are slightly browned and seared. Serve over rice. Leftover sauce can be stored in an airtight container for up to 2 weeks in the refrigerator or 2 months in the freezer.

lasagna

This lasagna recipe is satisfying and decadent, filled with protein-rich nut cheese and rice lasagna pasta. It is also loaded with dark leafy greens, a variety of mushrooms, and tomatoes. The Swiss chard, spinach, and nuts make it an iron-rich dish. While this recipe uses packaged vegan cheese, you can always use the Herbed Soft Cheese (page 12) or Almond Feta Cheese (page 16). Serve with a side of simple white beans dressed in olive oil to make this a complete protein meal. Because the lasagna is so rich and flavorful, I recommend also serving a green salad as a lighter side dish and perhaps some rolls made from the Sandwich Bread (page 7).

Makes 8 servings

¼ cup arrowroot powder

3½ tablespoons extra-virgin olive oil, divided, plus more for oiling

⅓ cup stemmed, coarsely chopped fresh flat leaf parsley

1¼ cups store-bought grated vegan cheese, divided

2 cups Vegetable Stock (page 19)

Sea salt and freshly ground black pepper

1 large onion, finely chopped

2¼ cups thinly sliced mixed mushrooms (porcini, portobello, and morels)

4 cups fresh spinach, finely chopped

3 cups finely chopped Swiss chard

⅛ to ¼ teaspoon freshly grated nutmeg

3 cloves garlic, minced

3 tablespoons tomato puree

1 (28-ounce) can chopped tomatoes

12 sheets precooked rice lasagna pasta

1. To make the cheese sauce, in a medium saucepan over low heat, whisk the arrowroot with 1 tablespoon of the oil continuously for 5 minutes. Add the parsley, ½ cup of the cheese, and the stock. Simmer while whisking, for 2 to 3 minutes more, until thick and creamy. Season to taste with salt and pepper and remove from the heat.

2. In a large skillet over medium heat, heat 1½ tablespoons of the oil. Sauté the onion and mushrooms until the onion becomes transparent and just starts to brown, about 6 minutes. Add the spinach and chard and cook until the greens wilt but are still a vibrant green, about 1½ minutes. Season to taste with salt, pepper, and nutmeg. Set aside.

3. To make the tomato sauce, in a large skillet (you may need to transfer the mushroom mixture to a large bowl if you don't have another large skillet) over medium-low heat, heat the remaining 1 tablespoon oil and sauté the garlic until it has just begun to brown and is very fragrant, about 3 minutes. Add the tomato puree and chopped tomatoes. Simmer until the sauce thickens, just over 10 minutes.

4. Preheat the oven to 400 degrees F. Lightly oil a 9-by-13-inch ovenproof dish. Spread half of the tomato sauce over the bottom and cover with a single layer of pasta. Spread one-third of the cheese sauce over the pasta, then half of the mushroom mixture. Cover with a layer of pasta. Cover with the rest of the red sauce. Add the second layer of cheese sauce, followed by the rest of the mushroom mixture. Add the final layer of pasta. Top with the remaining cheese sauce. Sprinkle the remaining ¾ cup cheese over the top. Bake for 30 minutes and serve while piping hot.

You can double this recipe and freeze one of the lasagnas to enjoy after a busy day or when you have guests coming. To do so, make the lasagna that is to be frozen in a glass or ceramic baking dish. Follow all the steps, assembling the lasagna right up to the baking point. Put the unbaked lasagna in the refrigerator for an hour before wrapping it for the freezer. Wrap it at least twice with freezer-safe plastic wrap and then with aluminum foil. The lasagna can be frozen for up to 3 months. Plan ahead when you are going to bake the lasagna, as it will need to thaw in the refrigerator for 24 hours before baking. To prepare, remove the foil and plastic wrap, cover again with the foil, and bake in a preheated 400 degree F oven for 40 minutes. Remove the foil for the last 10 minutes of baking.

wild chanterelle mushrooms on polenta rounds

You may be surprised to know that wild chanterelles contain all the essential amino acids, offering a complete protein! Chanterelle mushrooms are seasonal, so if you fancy this dish when chanterelles are out of season, you can substitute other wild or domestic mushrooms. Dried porcini mushrooms are easy to come by and can be reconstituted in water in a half hour's time. Shiitake mushrooms are another good substitute. Button mushrooms are the most economical while still providing excellent texture and carrying the flavors of the herbs, white wine, and garlic.

Makes 4 to 6 servings

¾ cup coarse-grind cornmeal

¼ cup amaranth

¼ teaspoon sea salt, plus more
　for seasoning

3 cups water

Freshly ground black pepper

3 tablespoons canola or extra-virgin
　olive oil, plus more for oiling
　and brushing

4 cloves garlic, finely chopped

1½ pounds chanterelle or other
　mushrooms, brushed clean, cut
　into ¼-inch slices

⅓ cup white wine

1 cup cooked white navy beans,
　or 1 cup from 1 (15-ounce) can,
　rinsed and drained

1½ cups cherry tomatoes, halved

1½ teaspoons chopped fresh thyme

1½ teaspoons chopped
　fresh oregano

1. In a medium saucepan over low heat, combine the cornmeal, amaranth, and salt. Slowly whisk in the water. Increase the heat to medium-high and bring the polenta to a light boil. Immediately reduce the heat to low and continue cooking, whisking often. Cook until the polenta is thick but still pourable, about 12 minutes. Season to taste with pepper.

2. Line a baking sheet with parchment paper and lightly oil. Pour the polenta onto the baking sheet and spread it out evenly, about ½ inch thick, with an offset spatula. (The polenta may not reach the sides of the baking sheet.) Brush the top with oil and cover with wax paper or plastic wrap. Put the polenta in the refrigerator to set, about 3 hours (or prepare ahead of time and refrigerate until the next day).

3. To bake the polenta, preheat the oven to 375 degrees F. Lightly oil a baking sheet. Using a round 1½-inch-diameter cookie cutter, cut out 12 rounds (or slice into small squares or diamonds). Transfer the polenta onto the baking sheet. Brush each one with additional oil and bake for 25 minutes.

4. Meanwhile, prepare the mushroom topping. In a large pan over medium heat, heat the oil. Add the garlic and gently sauté for 3 minutes. Add the mushrooms and cook, stirring occasionally, until they slightly brown, just under 10 minutes. Add the wine, beans, tomatoes, thyme, and oregano, reduce the heat to low, and cook until the wine is absorbed into the mushrooms and any excess liquid has cooked off. Season to taste with salt and pepper. Place a spoonful of the mushroom mixture on top of each polenta round and serve.

quinoa and red bean timbales

This dish has a mild, sweet hint of spice with delightful textures from the currants and pine nuts interspersed throughout the high-protein quinoa and red beans. The red beans, amaranth, and pine nuts all provide iron, and the red beans offer more antioxidants than any other food—plus their fiber regulates blood sugar long after the meal. For kids, this really makes a difference for lasting energy and stable moods. I find that with quinoa it's best to use small ramekins to form the timbales; the circular shape holds up better. The Chinese Green Beans (page 98) and the Carrot Ginger Bisque (page 84) go well with this dish.

Makes 6 to 8 servings

1½ tablespoons extra-virgin olive oil,
   plus more for oiling
4 shallots, finely chopped
1½ teaspoons ground cumin
½ teaspoon ground cinnamon
½ teaspoon ground curry
4 tablespoons pine nuts
1 cup quinoa, rinsed and drained
   (unless sprouted)
¼ cup amaranth
2⅛ cups water

½ cup currants
⅓ cup chopped fresh tomatoes
¾ teaspoon sea salt, plus more
   for seasoning
¾ cup cooked small red beans,
   or ¾ cup from 1 (15-ounce) can,
   rinsed and drained
3 tablespoons finely chopped fresh
   flat leaf parsley
Freshly ground black pepper

1. Lightly oil 6 to 8 small ramekin molds.

2. In a large sauté pan over medium heat, heat the oil and add the shallots. Sauté until they soften and just begin to brown, about 4 minutes. Add the cumin, cinnamon, curry, and pine nuts. Sauté for another minute, then add the

quinoa, amaranth, water, currants, tomatoes, and salt. Bring to a boil. Immediately reduce the heat to low, cover, and cook until all the water has been absorbed and the quinoa is fluffy, about 15 to 20 minutes. Stir in the beans and parsley. Season to taste with salt and pepper. Fill the ramekins to the brim in order to mold the mixture into timbales, and turn out onto serving plates.

> For a more casual dish that travels well, skip the timbale-forming part of this recipe. Present the dish in a serving platter or bowl. Cover with foil and take to your next potluck or picnic. A beautiful garnish is a few sprigs of fresh thyme or any green in your vegetable beds that has bolted—that is, has sent up a tall stalk and flowered. Rapini produces beautiful yellow flowers that are nutty tasting.

delicata squash and pesto-dressed white beans with sun-dried tomatoes

This dish is vibrant with color and really full-flavored with a lavish portion of pesto. It is a terrific choice for a potluck or picnic, because it's easy to transport and serve, and it tastes fantastic at room temperature. The beans and pesto provide ample protein and loads of fiber. The delicata squash is very high in vitamin A, and the garlic and basil in the pesto support the immune system. To make this a meal with complete protein, serve with the Quinoa Flatbread (page 8). Good side-dish choices include the Bok Choy with Seeds (page 100) and the Broccolini with Italian Flair (page 102).

Makes 4 servings

1½ cups fresh basil leaves

½ cup extra-virgin olive oil

1 cup pine nuts, divided

½ cup walnuts

6 cloves garlic

¼ cup nutritional yeast

¾ teaspoon sea salt, plus more for seasoning

½ teaspoon freshly ground black pepper, plus more for seasoning

2 medium delicata squashes

1½ cups cooked white navy beans, or 1 (15-ounce) can, rinsed and drained

½ cup loosely packed finely chopped fresh flat leaf parsley

12 oil-packed sun-dried tomatoes, thinly sliced

1. To make the pesto, in a food processor fitted with the steel blade, process the basil, oil, ½ cup of the pine nuts, the walnuts, garlic, nutritional yeast, salt, and pepper to a coarse (but not a smooth) consistency. Season to taste with additional salt and pepper.

2. To prepare the squashes, scrub them well (the skin is edible). Slice in half lengthwise and scoop out the seeds. Cut into ¼-inch-thick half-moons. In a large pan, cover the squash with water and steam, covered, over high heat until tender, about 10 minutes. Check periodically and add more water if necessary so the squash (and the pan) doesn't scorch. Transfer the squash with a slotted spoon to a large bowl. Add the beans, pesto, and parsley and toss well. Season to taste with salt and pepper. Sprinkle with the tomatoes and the remaining ½ cup pine nuts and serve.

tamale pie

This luscious layered pie is lightly spiced to accommodate a child's taste buds while being full of flavor to satisfy the entire family. Combining black beans with polenta offers complete protein, and the abundant vitamin C in the vegetables increases absorption of the iron in the spinach and black beans. Those seeking a bit of a kick with this meal can add a splash of hot sauce!

Makes 8 servings

2 tablespoons extra-virgin olive oil, plus more for oiling

1 onion, diced

2 shallots, finely chopped

2 teaspoons chile powder

1 zucchini, halved and thinly sliced into half-moons

2 tomatoes, diced

1 orange bell pepper, seeded and diced

2 cups chopped butternut squash, or 1 (10-ounce) frozen package

1½ cups cooked black beans, or 1 (15-ounce) can, rinsed and drained

4 cups cold water, divided

1½ cups medium-grind cornmeal

¼ cup amaranth

¼ cup quinoa

2 teaspoons kosher salt, divided

6 cups baby spinach

1 tablespoon chopped fresh oregano

Pico de Gallo (page 21), for serving

1 avocado, sliced, for serving

1. In a large sauté pan over medium heat, heat the oil and sauté the onion, shallots, and chile powder until the onions are transparent, about 5 minutes. Add the zucchini and sauté until it begins to brown, about 5 minutes. Add the tomatoes, bell pepper, squash, and beans. Continue to cook over medium-low heat for 10 minutes.

2. Meanwhile, preheat the oven to 350 degrees F and lightly oil a 10-inch springform pan. In a large pot, bring 3 cups of the water to a boil. In a medium bowl, combine the cornmeal, amaranth, quinoa, and 1 teaspoon of the salt with the remaining 1 cup water. Slowly pour the polenta mixture into the pot, stirring constantly. Reduce the heat to low and simmer, continuing to stir, until the polenta is thick and stiff, about 7 minutes.

3. Add the spinach, the remaining 1 teaspoon salt, and the oregano to the vegetable mixture. Stir to combine well.

4. In the springform pan, layer a third of the polenta to form the base of the tamale pie. Follow with half of the vegetable mixture. Add another third of the polenta, using a spatula to spread it evenly. Cover with the remaining vegetable mixture. Top with the last third of the polenta. Smooth the surface with the spatula and bake until the vegetable mixture is bubbling around the edges and the polenta is just lightly browned, about 1 hour. Serve wedges of tamale pie with pico de gallo and avocado.

black bean burgers

These burgers go with the Sweet Potato Oven Fries (page 112) like jam goes with toast! The fries can also be made with yams. These burgers have many of the attributes of the Red Bean Burgers (page 45), being high in fiber, protein, and iron as well as antioxidants. The Black Bean Burgers, however, are more assertive with chile spice flavor—but aren't too spicy. Be sure to have ketchup or aioli for dipping. For those who enjoy more heat, add a pinch of cayenne to the aioli.

Makes 4 servings

1 tablespoon plus 1 teaspoon
   extra-virgin olive oil, plus more
   for oiling
⅓ cup diced yellow onion
½ cup peeled diced carrot
½ cup diced red bell pepper
¼ cup finely chopped mushrooms
1 tablespoon ground cumin
2 tablespoons chile powder
5 cloves garlic, minced
4 tablespoons tomato paste
1 tablespoon maple syrup
1½ tablespoons whole grain mustard
½ teaspoon kosher salt

1 cup cooked black beans,
   or 1 cup from 1 (15-ounce) can,
   rinsed and drained
½ cup cooked small red beans,
   or ½ cup from 1 (15-ounce) can,
   rinsed and drained
¾ cup gluten-free and vegan
   cracker crumbs (such as
   Mary's Gone Crackers)
8 slices Sandwich Bread (page 7)
1 avocado, sliced
4 slices large heirloom or
   beefsteak tomatoes
4 lettuce leaves
½ red onion, thinly sliced

1. In a small skillet over medium heat, heat the oil. Add the onion, carrot, bell pepper, mushrooms, cumin, and chile powder. Sauté until the vegetables soften, about 5 minutes. Add the garlic and stir briefly. Add the tomato paste, maple syrup, mustard, and salt. Stir to combine well and remove from the heat to cool until warm, about 10 minutes.

2. Preheat the oven to 450 degrees F and lightly oil a baking sheet.

3. When the vegetables are just warm, put them in the food processor along with the beans and cracker crumbs. Pulse a few times to combine, leaving the mixture chunky.

4. Form the bean mixture into 4 large patties. Put them on the baking sheet and bake for 20 minutes. Lightly toast the bread. Serve the patties between the slices of bread with avocado, tomato, lettuce, and onion.

sweets & treats

DESSERTS GIVE A MEAL the feeling of festivity, and children find them especially wonderful. I am delighted to be using predominantly dates and maple syrup as the sweeteners in these recipes (with the exception of one cookie—the Cashew Butter Shortbread (page 165)—which calls for coconut palm sugar). Many of the cookies are grain-free, made with ground walnuts or almonds. The cakes are the sweetest, made with more maple syrup than the other recipes. The Chocolate Pumpkin Seed Brittle (page 162) is an absolute must to make. It is deeply satisfying, and you can consider it a healthy snack when eaten in moderation. The popsicle recipes feel like an indulgent treat, while nourishing with some unsuspected ingredients like spinach and avocado.

oatmeal raisin cookies

These will most likely become a mainstay in your house. They taste like a special treat without being sugary; in fact, they are sweetened with Medjool dates, which provide a significant amount of potassium. And being made substantially of oats, the cookies are also full of fiber and protein.

Makes 12 cookies

1⅔ cups gluten-free oats, divided
⅓ cup almonds
½ teaspoon sea salt
½ teaspoon ground cinnamon
½ teaspoon baking soda

10 Medjool dates, pitted
¼ cup water
1 teaspoon vanilla extract
¼ cup coconut oil
½ cup raisins

1. Preheat the oven to 350 degrees F. Line a baking sheet with parchment paper (if you have no parchment, use the sheet without oiling). In a food processor fitted with the steel blade, pulse 1 cup of the oats, the almonds, salt, cinnamon, and baking soda to form a coarse flour. Transfer to a mixing bowl and set aside.

2. Put the dates, water, and vanilla in the food processor and puree until completely smooth. Add the oat mixture and oil to the food processor. Pulse until well combined and doughy. Return the dough to the mixing bowl and stir in the raisins and the remaining ⅔ cup oats.

3. Divide the dough into 12 portions and form them into balls. Place them on the baking sheet. Flatten each ball with your palm to form cookies with a 3 inch diameter. Bake until golden, about 15 minutes. Let the cookies rest on the baking sheet for 5 minutes and then transfer to a rack to cool. Cool the cookies completely before storing in an airtight container for up to 5 days in the refrigerator.

chocolate chip cookies

These scrumptious chocolaty cookies are grain-free, as the dough is made with nourishing ground almonds. Almonds provide absorbable, high-quality protein. One thing I love about making a cookie dough with almonds is their power to reduce blood sugar spikes after meals. For kids, especially, it is pretty terrific to have a cookie that doesn't produce a sugar high followed by a sugar low. Being sweetened with dates and dark chocolate, these cookies are delicious while providing steady, long-lasting energy.

Makes 12 cookies

2 cups raw almonds
10 Medjool dates, pitted
2 teaspoons vanilla extract
½ teaspoon kosher salt

3 tablespoons coconut oil
¼ cup water
3 ounces 85 percent dark chocolate, chopped into chip sizes

1. Preheat the oven to 325 degrees F. Line a baking sheet with parchment paper (if you have no parchment, use the sheet without oiling). In a food processor fitted with the steel blade, process the almonds and dates to a coarse crumbly mixture, about 1 minute. Add the vanilla, salt, and oil. Process for 30 seconds more to combine. Add the water and process for another 30 seconds. Transfer to a mixing bowl and stir in the chocolate with a wooden spoon.

2. Divide the dough into 12 portions and form them into balls. Place them on the baking sheet. Flatten each ball with your palm to form cookies with a 3 inch diameter. Bake until golden, about 15 minutes. Let the cookies rest on the baking sheet for 5 minutes and then transfer to a rack to cool. Cool the cookies completely before storing in an airtight container for up to 5 days in the refrigerator.

raspberry walnut thumbprint cookies

With its glistening, jewel-like jam center, this makes a festive holiday cookie—and it's grain-free, consisting primarily of walnuts, dates, and shredded coconut. Walnuts are a great source of omega-3 fatty acids and have more antioxidants than any other nut. If I know the cookies will all be eaten within one day, I'll use a fresh cherry half as the center. This makes a darling cookie that is even less sweet, but the cherry half doesn't keep as well as the jam center, so that version is best for an immediate gathering, not the cookie jar.

Makes 20 cookies

2 cups walnut halves
½ teaspoon kosher salt
12 Medjool dates, pitted
   and chopped
¼ cup water

1 teaspoon vanilla extract
1 cup unsweetened shredded
   coconut
Raspberry jam or other favorite
   jam or jelly

1. Preheat the oven to 350 degrees F. Line a baking sheet with parchment paper (if you have no parchment, use the sheet without oiling). In a food processor fitted with the steel blade, pulse the walnuts and salt to a coarse crumb, just shy of a flour. Transfer to a mixing bowl. Put the dates, water, and vanilla in the food processor and puree until completely smooth. Add the date mixture to the walnuts. Stir in the coconut until well combined.

2. Roll tablespoons of dough in your palm to create 1-inch balls and place them on the baking sheet. Make an indentation in each with your thumb. Place a ½ teaspoon of the jam in each indent. Bake until golden, about 15 minutes. Let the cookies rest on the baking sheet for 5 minutes and then transfer to a rack to cool. Cool the cookies completely before storing in an airtight container for up to 5 days in the refrigerator.

chocolate pumpkin seed brittle

One really cannot say too many good things about dark chocolate! Dark chocolate actually stimulates endorphin production, which in turn creates feelings of well-being. This decadent treat also features the goodness of pumpkin seeds, walnuts, and coconut, sweetened minimally with mineral-rich maple syrup. Best of all, it comes together quickly. When slicing the brittle, use a hot knife. If it does not slice easily at first, let it warm slightly on the counter at room temperature for fifteen to thirty minutes. The brittle may also be stored in the freezer in an airtight container to prolong its shelf life for up to one month.

Makes 16 servings

1 cup pumpkin seeds
1½ cups walnuts
⅓ cup unsweetened shredded
  coconut
8 ounces unsweetened chocolate

½ cup coconut oil
2 teaspoons vanilla extract
½ teaspoon kosher salt
3½ tablespoons maple syrup

1. Preheat the oven to 350 degrees F. Line a 10-inch square pan with parchment paper, leaving some overhang to aid in removing the brittle when it's done.

2. Spread the pumpkin seeds and walnuts on a baking sheet and toast in the oven for 10 minutes. Spread the coconut on another baking sheet and toast for 5 minutes. In a double boiler set over simmering water, melt the chocolate and oil to a smooth liquid. Remove from the heat and stir in the vanilla, salt, maple syrup, seeds, nuts, and coconut. Pour the mixture into the prepared pan, smooth over with a spatula, and freeze for 40 minutes. Remove the brittle by the edges of the parchment paper, chop into individual servings, and store in an airtight container in the refrigerator for up to 1 week.

peanut butter cookies

Peanut butter is a satisfying and abundant source of protein—and a complete protein when combined with gluten-free oats, as in these cookies. Sweetened with dates, they satisfy a sweet tooth without being overly sweet. The dark chocolate centers make them extra yummy while providing more antioxidants. Mix things up by replacing the peanut butter and nuts with almond butter and nuts.

Makes 15 cookies

1¼ cups gluten-free oat flour
¼ teaspoon sea salt
½ teaspoon baking soda
12 Medjool dates, pitted
   and chopped
⅓ cup canola oil
½ teaspoon vanilla extract

½ cup peanut butter or
   almond butter
½ cup dry roasted salted peanuts
   or almonds, chopped
1 (3-ounce) 85 percent dark
   chocolate bar, cut into
   15 squares

1. Preheat the oven to 350 degrees F. Line a baking sheet with parchment paper (if you have no parchment, use the sheet without oiling). In a small bowl, combine the flour, salt, and baking soda. Put the dates, oil, and vanilla in a food processor fitted with the steel blade and puree until completely smooth. Add the flour mixture and peanut butter to the food processor and pulse until well combined and smooth. Transfer to a mixing bowl and stir in the peanuts.

2. Roll tablespoons full of dough in your palm to create 1½-inch balls and place them on the baking sheet. Flatten each ball with your palm to form cookies with a 1½ to 2 inch diameter. Press a square of chocolate onto the top of each cookie. Bake until golden, about 15 minutes. Let the cookies rest on the baking sheet for 5 minutes and then transfer to a rack to cool. Cool the cookies completely before storing in an airtight container for up to 5 days in the refrigerator.

cashew butter shortbread

These delightful cookie-cutter cookies are a joy to make with kids. A roll-out dough like this one comes in handy for so many holidays and seasons. In the spring, we love to make butterfly shortbreads. For a frivolous and fancy affair, you might indulge in decorating these with sprinkles. Health food stores offer some nice ones that are colorful, yet made without artificial food coloring. The main flour in this dough is buckwheat flour, which not only slows down the rate of glucose absorption, but also provides a complete protein.

Makes 12 cookies

1 cup buckwheat flour
½ cup brown rice flour, plus more
    for rolling
½ teaspoon baking soda
¼ teaspoon kosher salt

½ cup canola oil
⅓ cup coconut palm sugar
1 teaspoon vanilla extract
½ cup cashew butter

1. Preheat the oven to 375 degrees F. Line a baking sheet with parchment paper (if you have no parchment paper, use the sheet without oiling). In a medium bowl, combine the buckwheat flour, brown rice flour, baking soda, and salt. In a separate mixing bowl, combine the oil, sugar, vanilla, and cashew butter. Add the dry ingredients to the wet ingredients and stir to make a smooth dough.

2. On a generously floured surface, roll out the dough. Use your favorite cookie cutters to cut out shapes. Bake until golden, about 15 minutes. Let the cookies rest on the baking sheet for 5 minutes and then transfer to a rack to cool. Cool the cookies completely before storing in an airtight container for up to 5 days in the refrigerator.

brownies

These brownies are decadent in taste and healthy to boot. They are doubly chocolaty with cocoa powder and baking chocolate. It is the flavonols in chocolate that make it so spectacular, health-wise. The flavonoids in cocoa actually increase blood flow to the brain, which in turn increases brain cognition. These brownies are sweetened with dates and maple syrup. You know that sweets should be consumed in moderation; that said, when you do enjoy sweets, it's nice to use sweeteners with trace minerals, such as maple syrup. If you feel like going all out, frost the brownies with the Dark Chocolate Ganache Frosting (page 177).

Makes 8 servings

½ cup coconut oil, plus more for oiling

Brown rice flour, for dusting

4 ounces unsweetened baking chocolate, chopped

12 Medjool dates, pitted

⅛ cup maple syrup

1 teaspoon vanilla extract

½ cup chickpea flour

½ cup cocoa powder, unsweetened

½ teaspoon sea salt

½ teaspoon baking soda

¾ cup walnuts, finely chopped

1. Preheat the oven to 350 degrees F. Prepare a 10-inch square pan by lightly oiling it and dusting with brown rice flour, or line it with parchment paper with extra overhang for easy removal.

2. In a double boiler set over simmering water, melt the chocolate. In a food processor fitted with the steel blade, puree the dates, oil, maple syrup, and vanilla until completely smooth. In a medium mixing bowl, sift together the chickpea flour, cocoa, salt, and baking soda. Add the wet ingredients to the dry ingredients and stir in the melted chocolate, combining until well blended. Fold in the chopped walnuts. Transfer the batter to the prepared baking pan. Bake until slightly firm to the touch, about 17 to 20 minutes. Let cool slightly before cutting and serving. Store the cooled brownies in an airtight container in the refrigerator for up to 5 days.

carrot cake

Carrot cake is beloved as a high-fiber, sweet, and tender dessert. This carrot cake recipe also delivers the benefits of brown rice flour and maple syrup, as well as the traditional carrots, pecans, coconut, and raisins. You can serve squares of a 9-by-13-inch sheet cake frosted or unfrosted—unfrosted, this is a fantastic coffee cake to bring to a brunch.

Makes 20 cupcakes, one 9-inch double-layer cake, or one 9-by-13-inch sheet cake

1 cup brown rice flour
½ cup gluten-free oat or tapioca flour
¾ teaspoon baking soda
½ teaspoon kosher salt
1 teaspoon ground cinnamon
½ cup canola oil
¾ cup water
2 teaspoons vanilla extract

1 cup maple syrup
¾ cup peeled grated carrots (about 2 medium carrots)
½ cup unsweetened shredded coconut
¾ cup finely chopped pecans
½ cup golden raisins
1 recipe German Maple Frosting (page 175)

1. Preheat the oven to 350 degrees F. Line 2 standard muffin tins with 20 cupcake liners, or line 2 (9-inch) cake pans or a 9-by-13-inch sheet cake pan with parchment paper cut precisely to fit the bottom of the pans.

2. In a medium bowl, combine the flours, baking soda, salt, and cinnamon. In another medium bowl, combine with the oil, water, vanilla, and maple syrup. Whisk the dry ingredients into the wet ingredients. Mix in the carrots, coconut, pecans, and raisins. Fill the muffin cups to about two-thirds full, or divide the batter equally between the

For cake decorating tricks and ideas, refer to Tips for Cooling, Assembling, and Frosting Layer Cakes (page 172).

two cake pans, or pour the batter into the sheet cake pan. Bake on the middle rack of the oven until the cake is golden and springs back when touched or a toothpick inserted in the center comes out with just a few crumbs attached. The cupcakes take 20 to 25 minutes, the layer cake takes about 35 minutes, and the sheet cake takes about 40 minutes.

3. When the cupcakes are cool, frost each one. For the layer cake, frost the top of each layer, stack them together, and frost the sides. For the sheet cake, frost the top. Serve and enjoy!

Another option for any of the cake or cupcake recipes is to make miniature cupcakes. These are perfect for a celebration at the end of a school day—a birthday party, for example. These adorable little cakes are fancy and celebratory while providing less of a sugar hit in the middle of the day. The cake recipes in this book, while substantially less sweet than the norm, will still give a surge of energy to little ones. Miniature cupcakes take only 10 to 12 minutes to bake and can be tested for doneness just like the larger cupcakes and cakes. To transport frosted cupcakes, pop them back into their baking tins to hold them securely in transit. The tins can be placed in a covered box; you can also stick toothpicks into the corner cupcakes to support a draping of plastic wrap.

strawberry amaretto cupcakes

These luscious cupcakes are meant for special occasions. They are our top choice for celebrations at classes or large gatherings, as it seems they are universally enjoyed (much to my surprise, I've learned that not everyone loves chocolate). Although the batter is sweeter than muffin batter, it can be made into lovely little muffins or cakes without the frosting. Go ahead and add blueberries, raspberries, or even small pieces of banana to the batter before baking. One cup of fruit will do the trick; just increase the baking time by five minutes.

Makes 20 cupcakes or one 9-inch double-layer cake

2½ cups brown rice flour

1 cup chickpea flour, sifted

2 teaspoons baking soda

½ teaspoon kosher salt

2 teaspoons ground cinnamon

⅔ cup canola oil

1 cup plus 4 tablespoons water

2 teaspoons vanilla extract

1 teaspoon almond extract

1½ cups maple syrup

1 recipe German Maple Frosting (page 175)

10 strawberries, halved

1. Preheat the oven to 350 degrees F. Line 2 standard muffin tins with 20 cupcake liners or line 2 (9-inch) cake pans with parchment paper cut precisely to fit the bottom of the pans. In a medium bowl, combine the flours, baking soda, salt, and cinnamon. In another medium mixing bowl, combine the oil, water, vanilla, almond extract, and maple syrup. Whisk the dry ingredients into the wet ingredients. Fill the muffin cups to about two-thirds full or divide the batter equally between the 2 cake pans. Bake on the middle rack of the oven until the cake is golden and springs back when touched or a toothpick inserted in the center comes out with just a few crumbs attached. The cupcakes take 20 to 25 minutes and the layer cake takes 25 to 30 minutes.

2. When the cupcakes are cool, frost each one and top with the strawberries. For the layer cake, frost the top of each layer, stack them together, frost the sides, and dot the top with the strawberries. Serve and enjoy!

TIPS FOR COOLING, ASSEMBLING, AND FROSTING LAYER CAKES

Cooling Cakes

When you plan to frost a cake, always wait until the cake is completely cooled. After the cakes bake, let them rest in their pans for fifteen to twenty minutes (this is longer than the standard ten minutes but important with gluten-free cakes). Run a butter knife around the edge of the pan to loosen the cake from the sides; top the cake with an upside-down wire rack and while holding the pan rim and rack together, gently turn over so the cake drops out onto the rack for further cooling. A parchment paper lining allows for easy removal of the cake from the pan and is easily peeled from the cake once positioned on the rack to cool. I recommend letting the cakes cool for three hours before frosting.

I actually like to frost cakes when they are frozen because I know they won't break. If you also want to try this method, bake the cakes the day before needed (or several days, for that matter), and wrap the cooled cakes snugly in plastic wrap and again with foil. Freeze for at least eight hours. When ready to frost, remove the wrapping and get to it! Let the frosted cake thaw for at least six hours before serving.

Assembling Cakes

When it comes to frosting, it helps to elevate the cake above the counter for a good look at your work. You can use either a cake stand or a mixing bowl turned upside down with the cake plate resting securely on top. Put the first cake, bottom side up, on the plate or platter. Tuck pieces of wax paper or parchment paper around the cake to catch any frosting spills; when done, you can gently pull away the papers for a clean and professional look.

Frosting Cakes

Top the first layer with a large dollop of frosting (about one cup). Spread this over the cake with an offset spatula if you have one, otherwise a butter knife will suffice. Spread it out in concentric circles, letting some of the frosting extend just beyond the edge. Next, place the second layer, bottom side down, on top of the first. Put an even bigger dollop of frosting (about one and one-half cup) on top of this one. Spread the frosting evenly, rotating the bowl or cake stand. Leaving the frosting thicker on top prevents spots where cake crumbs can stick to the frosting. The frosting that overhangs will be used to finish the sides. Frost the sides in sections, making it your goal to first cover the cake minimally before smoothing out with additional frosting or creating artistic waves. Lastly, either smooth the sides with the offset spatula or create waves or swirls with a butter knife.

Piping Frosting and Writing Messages

The Dark Chocolate Ganache Frosting (page 177) is a fun one to pipe. The German Maple Frosting (page 175) doesn't lend itself well to piping due to the texture. The most important thing to remember with the chocolate frosting is that *temperature is everything*. This frosting is at its best if it is allowed to cool on the counter until set—that is, thickened to frosting consistency—rather than the refrigerator. The refrigerator will likely make the frosting thicken unevenly, with solid chunks, but this can be worked out; it just means ever so slightly reheating a small portion of it over a double boiler and whipping it with the remaining frosting in a stand mixer to smooth out any chunks. The ideal consistency is a smidgen less thick than traditional cream cheese frosting.

(continued)

To pipe, I recommend filling a piping bag fitted with your favorite decorative tip about one-half full. Gently twist the top portion of the bag tightly at the point to which the frosting is filled. Secure your hand around the twist and gently squeeze the bag to pipe out your favorite patterns.

Writing messages over cakes frosted with the maple or chocolate frostings works really nicely. Fit the piping bag with the writing tip and have a go. It never hurts to practice on wax paper first. Cursive is easier than printing, as the writing is continuous. For writing a message on a dark chocolate cake, cashew butter thinned with a smidgen of warmed coconut oil and whipped before scooping into the piping bag makes a cream-colored "frosting" that stands out in contrast to the rich dark-brown chocolate.

german maple frosting

This frosting is one of my favorites to work with because it comes together so easily and isn't too sensitive to temperature. I love the subtle sweetness of the maple syrup and the satisfying texture of the shredded coconut and chopped pecans. This frosting is intended to be spread with the aid of a butter knife or cake spatula; it does not lend itself well to piping.

Makes enough frosting for 16 cupcakes or one 9-inch double-layer cake

1¼ cups coconut oil

½ cup maple syrup

⅛ teaspoon kosher salt

1½ teaspoons vanilla extract

1¾ cups unsweetened shredded coconut, toasted and cooled

⅔ cups finely chopped toasted pecans

1. In the bowl of a stand mixer fitted with the paddle attachment (or in a mixing bowl by hand), combine all of the ingredients and whip until fluffy and thoroughly blended. The frosting can be stored in an airtight container in the refrigerator for up to 4 days. Before using, bring the frosting to room temperature by slightly warming over a double boiler and mix again.

dark chocolate cake

The chocolaty goodness in this cake comes from cocoa powder. To really reap the health benefits of cocoa, try to buy raw cocoa, as it is minimally processed. The German Maple Frosting (page 175) tastes phenomenal on this cake, but if you are a die-hard fan of chocolate, definitely stick with the heavenly Dark Chocolate Ganache Frosting (page 177).

Makes 18 cupcakes or one 9-inch double-layer cake

1¾ cups brown rice flour

¾ cup gluten-free oat or
   tapioca flour

¾ cup sifted cocoa powder

2 teaspoons baking soda

½ teaspoon kosher salt

½ cup plus 2 tablespoons canola oil

1 cup water

2 teaspoons vanilla extract

1 cup maple syrup

1 recipe Dark Chocolate Ganache
   Frosting (recipe follows)

1. Preheat the oven to 350 degrees F. Line 2 standard muffin tins with 18 cupcake liners or line 2 (9-inch) cake pans with parchment paper cut precisely to fit the bottom of the pans.

2. In a medium bowl, combine the flours, cocoa, baking soda, and salt. In another medium mixing bowl, combine the oil, water, vanilla, and maple syrup. Whisk the dry ingredients into the wet ingredients. Fill the muffin cups to about two-thirds full or divide the batter equally between the 2 cake pans. Bake on the middle rack of the oven until the cake springs back when touched or a toothpick inserted in the center comes out with just a few crumbs attached. The cupcakes take 18 to 20 minutes and the layer cake takes about 35 minutes.

For cake decorating tricks and ideas, refer to Tips for Cooling, Assembling, and Frosting Layer Cakes (page 172).

3. When the cupcakes are cool, frost each one. For the layer cake, frost the top of each layer, stack them together, and frost the sides. Serve and enjoy!

dark chocolate ganache frosting

This is my absolute favorite frosting! It is temperamental when it comes to the temperature at which it is easiest to work. If you have the time to let it set up on the counter rather than speeding up the process in the fridge, that is ideal. You can make the frosting in the morning and leave it on the kitchen counter all day to set. Try adding one teaspoon of peppermint extract along with the vanilla extract for a sensational chocolate mint frosting.

Makes enough frosting for 16 cupcakes or one 9-inch double-layer cake

½ cup coconut oil

2⅔ cups semisweet or bittersweet dairy-free dark chocolate (about 8 ounces), chopped

½ cup maple syrup

½ cup water

¼ teaspoon kosher salt

2 teaspoons vanilla extract or cognac

1. In a double boiler set over simmering water, melt the oil and chocolate. Remove the top pot and whisk in the maple syrup, water, salt, and vanilla. Keep whisking until the consistency thickens and the water is completely incorporated.

2. The frosting needs to set as it cools before it can be worked with. Let it sit on the counter for 4 hours, whisking occasionally. Once the frosting is set, whip it in a stand mixer fitted with the paddle attachment to break up any overly solidified chocolate. You can also speed up the setting process by placing the frosting in the refrigerator, but if it gets too cold, you will need to warm it again slightly and rewhip it. The frosting can be stored in an airtight container in the refrigerator for up to 4 days. Before using, bring the frosting to room temperature by slightly warming over a double boiler and mix again.

strawberry surprise popsicles

These popsicles have a surprising ingredient—cucumber! Cucumber not only adds a refreshing note, but it's a good source of B vitamins. Strawberries contain vitamin C in great abundance. Try throwing some basil in with the mint for an even brighter flavor.

Makes 6 popsicles

3 cups fresh strawberries
1 cup chopped peeled cucumber
⅛ cup maple syrup

3 tablespoons freshly squeezed
   lemon juice
½ cup fresh mint leaves
½ cup water

1. In a high-powered blender or food processor, blend all the ingredients until completely smooth. Pour the mixture into 6 popsicle molds and freeze for at least 3 hours.

world's healthiest popsicles

I just love that these popsicles contain avocado and spinach. This is a parent's rather sneaky way of bringing even more greens into their children's diet. After you blend up the ingredients, before pouring into the popsicle molds, taste the mixture to determine if the sweetness level is just right for your family. If not, add a tablespoon more of maple syrup, blend again, and freeze.

Makes 6 popsicles

1 avocado

2 cups baby spinach

1 cup frozen blueberries

1 banana

3 tablespoons raw cocoa

3 tablespoons maple syrup

1 teaspoon vanilla extract

1 cup water

1. In a high-powered blender or food processor, blend all the ingredients until completely smooth. Pour the mixture into 6 popsicle molds and freeze for at least 3 hours.

ACKNOWLEDGMENTS

Thank you, Joseph and Lillian, for you manifest a special magic in my life. Thank you, Mom, Dad, Kat, Malcolm, Jer, Leon, Jules, Andy, Rosie, Josh, Sherry, and Caleb. All of your love and support is deeply felt. Thank you to the generous community of friends who tested this collection of recipes. Thank you to the entire Sasquatch Books team! Thank you, Susan Roxborough, for seeing this book through; it was a true feat. Thank you, Em Gale, for your thorough insights and cheer. Thank you, Michelle Hope Anderson, for your direction early on in the creative process. Thank you, Charity Burggraaf, your photography brings a gorgeous quality to this book that I am most grateful for. Thank you, Julie Hopper, your culinary artistry and vision make for mouthwatering photos. Thank you, Anna Goldstein, for your design brilliance, once again. Thank you, Joyce Hwang, for your beautiful illustrations that create such a welcoming feel to the book. Thank you to the loving community I live in that surrounds me with meaningful and joyful connections.

INDEX

Note: Photographs are indicated by *italics*.

CONVERSIONS

VOLUME			LENGTH		WEIGHT	
UNITED STATES	**METRIC**	**IMPERIAL**	**UNITED STATES**	**METRIC**	**AVOIRDUPOIS**	**METRIC**
¼ tsp.	1.25 ml		⅛ in.	3 mm	¼ oz.	7 g
½ tsp.	2.5 ml		¼ in.	6 mm	½ oz.	15 g
1 tsp.	5 ml		½ in.	1.25 cm	1 oz.	30 g
½ Tbsp.	7.5 ml		1 in.	2.5 cm	2 oz.	60 g
1 Tbsp.	15 ml		1 ft.	30 cm	3 oz.	90 g
⅛ c.	30 ml	1 fl. oz.			4 oz.	115 g
¼ c.	60 ml	2 fl. oz.			5 oz.	150 g
⅓ c.	80 ml	2.5 fl. oz.			6 oz.	175 g
½ c.	125 ml	4 fl. oz.			7 oz.	200 g
1 c.	250 ml	8 fl. oz.			8 oz. (½ lb.)	225 g
2 c. (1 pt.)	500 ml	16 fl. oz.			9 oz.	250 g
1 qt.	1 l	32 fl. oz.			10 oz.	300 g

TEMPERATURE

OVEN MARK	FAHRENHEIT	CELSIUS	GAS		
				11 oz.	325 g
Very cool	250–275	130–140	½–1	12 oz.	350 g
Cool	300	150	2	13 oz.	375 g
Warm	325	165	3	14 oz.	400 g
Moderate	350	175	4	15 oz.	425 g
Moderately hot	375	190	5	16 oz. (1 lb.)	450 g
	400	200	6	1½ lb.	750 g
Hot	425	220	7	2 lb.	900 g
	450	230	8	2¼ lb.	1 kg
Very hot	475	245	9	3 lb.	1.4 kg
				4 lb.	1.8 kg

ABOUT THE AUTHOR

JENNIFER KATZINGER and her father first opened the doors of the Flying Apron Bakery in 2002, recognizing the value in gluten-free and vegan whole foods years in advance of what has become a rapidly expanding industry. After growing the bakery from a tiny takeout window in Seattle's University District to a spacious, lovely café in the city's Fremont neighborhood, Jennifer sold the bakery in 2010, and it continues to thrive.

After selling the bakery, Jennifer pursued her two greatest passions—being a mother and continuing to develop delicious, healthy recipes. She is delighted to bring you her sixth cookbook, a wonderful collection of recipes made with gluten-free and vegan ingredients.

Jennifer earned her BA in English Literature from the University of Washington and pursued a Masters in Industrial Design from Pratt Institute in Brooklyn, New York. She lives in Seattle with her husband, Joseph, their daughter, Lillian, and their dog, Neve. They enjoy taking long walks through beautiful parks of the Pacific Northwest and creating delicious, nurturing food together.